the modern
goddess'
guide to life

*how to be
absolutely divine
on a daily basis*

the modern goddess' guide to life

guide to

francesca de grandis

SOURCEBOOKS, INC.®
NAPERVILLE, ILLINOIS

Material in this book has appeared, perhaps in different form, in: The Third Road® training material; *The Wiccan and Faerie Grimoire of Francesca De Grandis* (an online publication); and in presentations—live, and on radio and television—throughout the United States. The Third Road® is a registered service mark owned by F. De Grandis.

This volume's stories and characters are fictional, and resemblances to persons living or dead are merely coincidental. The two following exceptions hold: the author herself is as real as she can manage; a few true tales within are about people who gave their permission.

This book is not a substitute for psychological treatment or for medical care by a physician. Users of this book are responsible for the results of their usage of the book's program and of products and services suggested.

Published by Sourcebooks, Inc.

P.O. Box 4410, Naperville, Illinois 60567-4410

(630) 961-3900

FAX: (630) 961-2168

www.sourcebooks.com

Library of Congress cataloging-in-Publication Data

De Grandis, Francesca.
  The modern goddess' guide to life / by Francesca De Grandis.
    p. cm.
  ISBN 1-4022-0165-6 (alk. paper)
  1. Women—Conduct of life. 2. Goddesses—Miscellanea. I. Title.
BJ1610.D4 2004
201'.43—dc22

                              2004000596

Printed and bound in the United States of America

ED 10 9 8 7 6 5 4 3 2 1

Other books by Francesca De Grandis

Be a Goddess! A Guide to Celtic Spells and Wisdom
for Self-Healing, Prosperity, and Great Sex

Goddess Initiation: A Practical Celtic Program for
Soul-Healing, Self-Fulfillment, and Wild Wisdom

Dedicated to the Pink Bunny Tribe

Table of Contents

the modern goddess' guide to life

the modern goddess' guide to life

all fun
and light
and
power

I believe we are put on this planet for two reasons: to have great sex and to help other people. (A friend of mine says we can do both at once, but that is not what I mean. Though she *does* have a point.)

What I *do* mean is that the Great Mother of Us All is, well, a mom, The Great Mom! And like all great moms she wants her kids to be happy. In fact, like all good mothers, she *really really* wants this for us.

She also wants us all to get along, and help each other, as brothers and sisters. Remember when you were little and your mother told you, "Don't be selfish"?

Okay, maybe that wasn't a good example because for all I know she was guilt-tripping you. In which case, let me tell you: the Great Mom would have said "It's okay to want some things just for yourself."

But she also tells us all that we can't be happy unless we, in addition, help others. That may mean helping your family, community, or the entire world.

And we shouldn't have to choose between being happy and helping other people be happy.

So this book is a fun way to do two things:

✳ Empower our own joy, and enjoy fabulous prizes—yup, these games and quizzes have prizes like more self-confidence, better communication skills, self-esteem, better sex, career success, and more. You don't even have to guess which door the best prize is behind.

✳ Increase our ability to serve our family, friends, and everyone else without being doormats or otherwise being unhappy about it.

Or as I always say, "Have great sex and help others!"

Fun is a remarkable healer and a profound gateway into our ability to create ourselves anew. Laughter helps us forget our fears long enough to stretch past our limits just a little bit more. Fun inspires us, uplifts us, and reminds us that life is worth living, risks are worth taking, and little pleasures can help us through our daily ups and downs as well as through our major challenges. Mind you, I am talking simple, unadorned, unpretentious, straight-ahead entertainment. Just enjoying a few laughs.

Let the games begin.

the modern goddess' guide to life

what the
heck is in
this
book?

*T*he Modern Goddess' Guide to Life consists of games and quizzes that are, I admit, irreverent. Thoroughly! I hope they also will bring a bit of light and good cheer to you. So, curl up, get comfy, and settle in; we'll share some secret chuckles. I've also thrown in a few bits of advice and life-strategies that I've come up with over the years. Whether you enjoy this book alone or with friends, think of it as a pajama party, Goddess style. My hope is that we have all the laughs, fun, and female bonding of a coffee klatch, raised to the divine level of self-help heaven. The games, if they need any props, usually use things that are already on hand.

This book will take you on an original adventure that provides insight into how fabulous you are, how wise, how powerful. And you'll see that, for a Goddess—and every woman *is* a Goddess—the world can be fun, rich, and filled with human warmth. When women convene we are practical and sassy when it comes to everything from career success to men to personal growth to in-laws to politics. And what better way to deal with all those topics than being our Goddess selves every step of the way?

Extraordinary times require extraordinary Goddesses—the historical Goddesses are great, but here are thirteen of the contemporary Goddesses who thrive in today's world, such as, to name a few, the Mother Goddess, Sex Goddess, Bad Girl Goddess, and Goddess-Just-Wants-To-Have-Fun. You'll also learn which Goddess you are. Each Goddess represents a given woman's unique abilities, as well as her own special style and flair.

Because a woman has within her all powers, you may discover you are more than one Goddess. In fact, the book gives you games that help you become any Goddess you need to be to get what you want out of life. Thus, on any given day or at any moment, you can shift into the divine being best suited to the situation at hand—whether it's a challenge or a chance to indulge.

Any reader of any religion or lack thereof, any person who pursues spirituality or doesn't, can enjoy using the word *Goddess* in this book as a metaphor, or perhaps even an archetype, to find, honor, and draw on her female power and thus increase that power to enrich life and make a difference in the world. An updated view of Goddesses reveals time-tested wisdoms for *anyone*. Terms like *Domestic Goddess* are mainstream now. We all know what they mean symbolically. I just saw a T-shirt for horse lovers with "Stable-Goddess" printed on it! And "Goddess Glitter" (sparkles for face and body) is readily available in the cosmetic section of my local drug store.

Goddesses are symbols of a woman's far-ranging assets. As such, they personify each woman's uniqueness; reveal her female wiles; and demonstrate that utterly feminine, steadfast resoluteness in the face of trials. A Goddess has integrity, moral virtue, purity of heart, depth of spirit. And using *Goddess* is an easy, fun way to get in touch with all that womanly power. For one thing, the word *Goddess* helps us delve into the touchy issues of gender and relationships with sensitivity and humor.

If you should happen to love a female deity as part of your religious practice—perhaps you embrace Wicca, Native American Shamanism, or a Goddess-oriented type of Buddhism—you already know there is enormous power available to a woman who knows she is a Goddess. This book might be an opportunity to share that wisdom with someone who's never understood before. This might be a way for them to grasp, and maybe even enjoy and benefit from, something that has already helped *you*. Yet they won't have to change their own spiritual beliefs or other views of life. Almost everyone relates to a modern usage of the word Goddess.

Having fun does not mean I am belittling or making light of Goddess religions or Goddess power. On the contrary, I'm writing with the long-respected tradition of sacred trickster/fool in mind. I hope this book in its own small way honors the Sacred Fool, the spiritual teacher and healer whose merriment has, historically speaking, revealed truth, whose barbs have exposed politicians' foibles, and whose jests have allowed us to laugh at ourselves. In laughing at ourselves, we learn to honestly self-examine, to love ourselves, shortcomings and all, and to cheerfully set about improving ourselves and the world we live in.

And for some spiritually-minded people, it is important to have that unique brand of silly, silly humor that is uplifting and joyful, and through which one pokes fun at oneself, yet does not *truly* belittle oneself in any way. So, use this book in any and every way you can think of. Here are a few examples:

* Don't frantically worry and scheme while waiting for your date to arrive. Take a long, leisurely bubble-bath, while you play a Sex Goddess game. When your date arrives, you'll be running the show.
* On coffee breaks, peruse the Corporate Goddess's secrets to get yourself amped up and overcome career challenges.
* Share the quizzes at parties for entertainment that makes a difference.
* Enjoy the games on the holidays to bring meaning to the occasion.
* Become an infamous hostess with ideal entertainment and party favors. Imagine what a girl's night out, wedding shower, or other soiree could turn into!

Though you'll see that what type of Goddess you are changes from day to day—maybe even from minute to minute—based on your moods, activities, immediate goals, etc., each woman tends to embody one or a few Goddess types when she looks at her life as a whole.

The Modern Goddess' Guide to Life portrays Goddesses that I suspect you will recognize not only in yourself but also in your friends and bosses, neighbors, and even archenemies. Women have immense powers, and an inner Goddess can symbolize these powers in a way that is true to our everyday way of life. A Goddess is in every women, all day long, doing the cooking, running the office, making sure the kids get off to school on time. Who but a Goddess could manage all that? When we realize this, we understand that our contributions to others are priceless. And once we get in touch with *some* of our Goddess power, we find it easier to increase it, bit by bit. We become bigger and better and happier and of more help to those we love and to the world. Use this book to have fun, worship yourself, and empower yourself.

Along with the games and quizzes, there are additional ways herein that will help you do these things. For example, reciting any or all of *A Goddess's Pledge (The "I'm Willing to Accept Diamonds As Homage" Manifesto)* on a coffee break, after a long day, or while brushing one's teeth, can be a real boost. And when your day is not feeling all that divine, that's even more the case!

After all, sister Goddess, the more powerful you get, the better a world it is for all of us!

what's a
nice
woman
like you
doing in a
book like
this?

I want to touch on a few serious points. (Picture me furrowing my brow—so that I look really intelligent—and nodding wisely as I talk to you. Or, if you prefer, imagine me how women *really* talk to one another—sitting in my pink flannel pajamas, waiting for my morning coffee to brew to kick-start my brain. In either case, here goes...)

This chapter is for those of us who are more serious-minded, or facing big challenges.

I love to work. But I love it so much that, sometimes, like many women, I forget about fun. And I forget that fun is one of the most effective healers and empowerments of all.

I'm an interfaith pastoral counselor and a traditional spiritual healer. For twenty years, through counseling, classes, writing, and special events—all geared toward inner change—I've helped people of all religions or no religion find personal satisfaction, follow their star, attain prosperity, and have a loving impact on the world.

Like other women, when someone comes to me with their problems, I buckle down and soberly get to business. It's my job to guide people through the inner and outer rocky terrains of life. I consider it a privilege. To have a profession in which I can also help people heal their inner blocks to happiness and service is a responsibility I take seriously. If a trauma survivor comes to me, it's no joke. But women can also have fun and get a huge amount of power *that* way—even the trauma survivor!

Straight-ahead celebration is sacred and meaningful and a viable way to radically improve your life. Women shouldn't have to feel one-dimensional.

You will never be fully self-realized if all you do is work at it: if there is not some joy and fun in the process, there will be no joy and fun resulting. The end is the means.

Both alternative and mainstream healers need to see the power of joy and games. Furthermore, if each of us participates in homespun spiritual activism, it helps each and every one of us to find our own no-nonsense, common sense brilliance, and humor will be shown to be an inevitable part of that. Joy and humor can heal and educate and empower.

Change *can* be hard work. I won't deny that. In my previous books I addressed the sort of change that demands that hard work. But fun and foolishness can also change you, and nowadays we might not give ourselves enough opportunity to let that happen. I know I haven't always. With this book, I am. *We* are.

The Goddess or any other loving deity loves fun. And when we embrace the joy divinely given us and just have a plain old good time, we can be amazed by the wonderful changes that occur in our psyches and our lives. Think of how uplifted you feel at a great concert. Your joy there can fill you with new determination and vitality. Fun can heal and empower us in ways nothing else might!

So feel confident that when you indulge in these quizzes and games you are nevertheless doing something important. This is a fun, humorous, *self-help* book.

Finally, here are a few quick bits of advice for those who need more solemn healing help than is generally found in this particular book.

If you need professional help, get it. (For information, see "Modern Resources for Modern Goddesses" on page 143.) Remember that a Goddess understands she sometimes needs help to feel happy and whole. She also asks for that support, if necessary mustering up the courage to do so.

People often think of professional help solely as therapists and psychiatrists. Yet unmanageable feelings, inability to move forward in one's life, and even trauma might be overcome by using a minister, rabbi, spiritual healer, psychic, shaman, or other pastoral counselor. None of these are substitutes for a therapist, but the opposite is also true. A counselor working in a spiritually or psychically based modality might be able to help you shift parts of yourself that a psychiatrist can't.

In the same vein, have you ever been, let's say, at the grocery store, and been reminded of something bad that happened to you and therefore needed to cry? And then felt overwhelmed, because you didn't know how to deal with your feelings?

That can happen anywhere, at any time. So of course it can happen in a Goddess game when you are finding your power, creating joy, and testing your limits of fun and pleasure. If you feel overwhelmed, take care of yourself.

When you were a little child, did you ever call "Time out"? Or "Olly, olly oxen free"?

Children understand that there can be a need to stop the game for a bit because something else important needs to happen. Always feel free to call time out or "Olly, olly oxen free." And then draw on your sister Goddesses for the love, cuddling, and talking that they can provide. Call your mom on the phone. Do what is needed to feel okay again so that you can, as would a child, start the games again full of pep and joy.

Now for some fun and humor (coupled with self-empowerment).

what
kind of
goddess
are you?

The Cosmic Spa for Goddesses

Imagine that in the other realm—in the land of fantasy and myth—there's a cosmic spa where a Goddess can kick back, indulge, frolic, and, lo, discover or rediscover her divine powers. These quizzes and games will take you there.

There is a Goddess within each of us, and there are many kinds of Goddess, each with her own unique powers. This chapter will help you discover which Goddess you are, or at least if you are embodying her at this particular moment. Since all women are truly, richly multifaceted, you get to enjoy being different Goddesses at different times in your life, perhaps even at different times in your day.

I've designated thirteen modern Goddesses and shown each one's strengths, each one's weaknesses, plus helpful hints for you when you're embodying the Goddess in question. Among those suggestions, you'll find everything from Fashion Ideas to How to Take Advantage of Your Cosmic Powers as a Deity, to Who Is Your Dream Date.

These being modern times, each Goddess has games she likes to play, listed at the end of her chapter. These are not only activities she especially enjoys but also games she likes leading Goddess galfriends in, which can be scads of fun. But wait, there's more! A Goddess's special games develop her specific powers even further—even a Goddess can get stronger—and if you are not the Goddess in question, you *can* be, by playing her games, which will lend you some of her style, strength, and savvy. Finally, okay, I'll admit it, the games are just fun! Every one for anyone. The actual games themselves are in the "Games for Goddesses" section that starts on page 115. You'll see from the lists for the various Goddesses that each game draws out the powers of several deities.

Be forewarned, these divinities' descriptions are *general* ideas of mine for you to use in deciding which divine powers you possess. So anyone who writes me saying, "I hate your Sex Goddess description. I am a very sexual woman and I don't in any way resemble what you describe," will be dubbed "Annoying Goddess Who Missed the Whole Point," the point being that my thumbnail sketches are jumping off points for you to adapt, throw out, or otherwise use to find the unique Goddess that *you* are! Sure I am giving quizzes to determine what type of Goddess you are, but if you answer "No" to all the descriptions of the Sex Goddess and still think you qualify, I am your biggest supporter!

All women are Goddesses. So, being a deity, you have all powers. Any name or title you choose is appropriate, and you can change your title as often as you want! If you thought changing clothes and hair styles was fun, imagine waking up, declaring yourself "Fount of Compassion and Understanding" and then, by lunch, deciding differently and becoming "She Who Doles Out Revenge Unto All Who Don't Like Her New Lipstick Color"!

…Okay, I shouldn't have made that last comment. Don't dole out revenge.

Be compassionate.

…Unless someone is really snide about your makeup.

And with that—enjoy being a Goddess!

The Quizzes

Since we shift who we are all day long—women are *so* versatile—the quiz for each Goddess can be used in one of two ways: either to discover whether you tend to live a life that by and large embodies the Goddess in question; or to learn if you are being her at the specific moment you are taking the quiz. So when you take the quiz, decide which way you feel like taking it right now. You can take it the other way later and do the quizzes as often as is powerful for you.

Each Goddess Quiz includes two fun and fabulous parts—a mini-quiz and a checklist.

The mini-quiz consists of two or three questions. Check off the box next to any questions you answer "yes."

When you want to discover if you are, let's say, a Corporate Goddess, go to her mini-quiz. Think of it as a pre-quiz: if you score poorly on that, save your time—there's no point in taking the rest of the quiz. Move on and take a quiz for another Goddess. But if you score highly enough, you might be a Corporate Goddess, and it's worth your time to take the full quiz to determine if you are, in fact, one. If your scores say you are, then go to her chapter and learn all sorts of ways to celebrate and increase your power.

If you do poorly on the mini-quiz and still think you might qualify as, to use the same example, a Corporate Goddess, take the full quiz anyway. You know best. And if you score poorly on *that*, I think the earlier chapters make it clear: decide on your own, according to your *own* guidelines, if you're a Corporate Goddess. And feel fully qualified, by decree of your own divine dictates, to proclaim yourself Corporate Goddess and proceed to her chapter, to use it as you will. I cannot emphasize strongly enough that ultimately *you* say what kind of Goddess you are.

In any case, after the pre-quiz you'll find the longer quiz, which consists of Goddess descriptions. Next to each description is a box to check off if the description fits you. Again, you either check off boxes next to statements that describe you overall, or, if you prefer, all the boxes that describe you right this minute.

However you score on any of the quizzes, all the Goddesses' chapters, as well as all the quizzes, are good for anyone to read. How else can you gain every power you might need unless you educate yourself about all the possibilities available to you as a Goddess? Whether you initially qualify or not via the quizzes, read up and play the games to be any Goddess you want!

Also, read up on all the Goddess-Gals so as to better understand your friends and enemies. You'll be more in control of your interactions.

Regarding taking the quizzes with a grain of salt: my girlfriend, Jane Lind, took all the full quizzes and scored only a couple of items per Goddess, not enough to fully qualify her for *any* of them. But I figure she's a little bit of every Goddess—a well-rounded, multi-faceted woman, like so many of us. So, take the quizzes just for fun—that's really what they're for—and remember that the scores, ultimately, are not what define you. As a matter of fact, in Jane's case, she is thoroughly, in a million ways, a Mother Goddess, and ditto a Sex Goddess, despite her low scores on their "tests." (Yes, despite popular opinion, one can be both a mother and a sexy babe!)

In addition, after each quiz is an interpretation of your score. You'll find that there are *degrees* to which a woman might be the Goddess in question. Good info to have so you know exactly where you stand.

There are two Goddesses whose chapters might be easy to miss because they don't need quizzes, since one is in *all* of us and the other is in most of us, at least once in our lifetime. The latter is the Goddess of Wrath and Unintentional Destruction. She is the aspect of ourselves that tries to change things for the better by, unfortunately, raising a ruckus that does more harm than good. We need to know how to spot this Goddess of Good Motives but of Unintended Harm when she appears in ourselves or others. Otherwise, we're in for trouble!

The other divinity without a quiz is the Ultimate Goddess, in some ways the most powerful deity in the modern world. Make sure you check out her chapter, because she is, well, the Ultimate Goddess.

Helpful Aside: If you find it hard to recognize yourself as a Goddess, whether it's as a particular type of Goddess or just a Goddess, period, here's a bit of advice I give my Goddess Spirituality students or *any* female client who might benefit from it: try a bubble bath. There's something about that sort of indulgence and pampering that tells us deep in our being that we're special, even divine. In addition to a soak in the tub, a facial and/or manicure deepens the "self-worship" we all deserve as women confronting the modern world.

To the quizzes!

The Mother Goddess Quiz

If your reply to a question is "Yes" or any variation thereof, for example, "Well, that's kind of like me," check the box next to that question.

❑ Do children immediately find their way onto your lap?
❑ Emotionally speaking, do adults? Do you dole out cookies and words of comfort to people regardless of their age—family members, strangers, even the clerk at the grocery store?

If you scored zero, hey! Maybe you never sit down so you don't *have* a lap. Go to another quiz. But if you scored one or two, you might be a Cosmic Mom. Move on to the rest of the quiz—try the check-list. You are a Mother Goddess if:

❑ You notice details that everyone else overlooks. Like whether all the children are back in the car after a rest stop.
❑ The night before Thanksgiving, you have a nightmare that the stuffing burns.
❑ No matter whom you're hugging, you absentmindedly pat their back as if you were burping them.
❑ You have a recipe for which you are "famous."
❑ When crossing the street next to another adult, you have to restrain yourself from grabbing their hand and seeing them safely across. (My

own mother once, much to my brother Roger's chagrin, snatched up his hand in hers when they were about to leave the curb. He was already old enough to *drive!*)

❑ You have a permanent groove across your tongue, from biting it! You know exactly how everything should be done, but you also know that no one will listen to you, anyway.

❑ You also know how to do laundry really well. You wish you didn't.

❑ Your favorite reading material is anything that can be read in the sixty-second pauses between life's comings and goings.

Count how many boxes you checked off, including your score from the mini-quiz.

The following is an interpretation of your tally. If you checked off only one or two items, don't worry. We all have our weak points, but we all also have our strong points. And they both wax and wane. Maybe you're a Sex Goddess, or a Sex Goddess *today*.

Scored three or four? You have enough mother potential that your own mother only tells you once or twice a month that you're breaking her heart.

If five to six of the items fit you, your mom is currently your best friend and the two of you swap mom-secrets.

Seven or eight, and this is the day that *Family Circle* needs you to send them helpful hints they can publish.

Nine to ten, and *Family Circle* needs you to mail them *yourself!* So that you can oversee the operation.

The Girlfriend Goddess Quiz

Check the box next to any question you can answer with "Yes":

❑ Is your shoulder always soggy from friends crying on it?

❑ Does everyone worship your unflagging loyalty?

If you answered "yes" even once, try the check-list below.

❑ Wherever you go, you carry a tiny sewing kit, extra pair of panty hose, and breath mints. And you never use them yourself. They're in case a friend has a button pop off, a run in her nylons, or an impromptu date.

❑ You would like a date. And if you met the perfect partner for yourself, you'd call your best friend to set the two of them up.

❑ Well, you wouldn't actually *mean* to set them up. But you would want them to meet. And then you would spend the entire visit helping them fall in love. Unintentionally.

❑ Your motto is "Friends before lovers. Because friends are forever. Lovers come and go."

❑ Last week, you went to a movie. The only reason for doing so is that your sister's boyfriend cancelled at the last minute and she wanted to prove her independence. It's not that sis doesn't seek out your company otherwise. You and she love to get together. But you won't go to a movie unless it's for a Samaritan reason. You're too busy.

❑ You're an expert on love. Well, this is true as long as you're not talking about your *own* love life.

❑ You have a deep and hidden longing to play the lead, so to speak, instead of the sidekick.

❑ Finally, you're just who you are—caring, sensitive, and often invisibly noble. And you know that, ultimately, that's all that counts.

Here's your Girlfriend Goddess rating, including the pre-quiz: If you checked off only one or two of the above boxes, your loyalty is given to a chosen few.

Check off three to five to be someone that other women can rely on.
Six to eight, and I want you as my best friend.

Finally, nine or ten, and either you're codependent—you're far too good a girlfriend—or you are what the Great Mother had in mind after She created the cosmos, then thought, "This isn't complete yet. I need a *sistah*!"

The Goddess of Love Quiz

Make a check mark in the box next to any question you answer in the affirmative, and you might be akin to the Goddess Venus:

❏ If you have no makeup on and just returned from a three-day camping trip without showers, are you nevertheless immediately recognized as the perfect object of worship and desire?

❏ Are you the glue that holds your family (workplace, community) together?

❏ Do you know just what to do to keep everyone's spirits high, tempers checked, and hearts cherished?

❏ Are your role models Gandhi, Eleanor Roosevelt, Martin Luther King Jr., and/or Jimmy Carter?

Score at least one of the above? Then finish the quiz!

❏ You think *bad* only refers to a mood, never to a person.

❏ When someone makes an unkind remark, even if it's, for example, terribly racist, you usually know how to admonish them in such a way that they feel supported and understood instead of attacked and ridiculed. And thus, you can help them change in a way they might not have if they had felt defensive.

❑ Your compassion, belief in humankind, and sensitivity draws romantic interest from many types of suitors.

❑ On your birthday, you receive cards from two of your exes, three business colleagues, your daughter's teacher, the checkout clerk that you met at your grocery store last week, and about thirty other people, all of whom think of you as their best friend.

❑ Love makes the world go 'round, and *you're* spinning the globe, *all day long*.

❑ And you don't mind doing it, it only seems natural and right; it makes you happy and content.

Including the results of the pre-quiz, score one or two and all is not lost—you do, at least, *have* a soul.

Check off three to five and you've a *shiny* soul, because of how well you treat everyone and how well they love you back.

Six to ten: you're a saint with sex appeal.

The Activist Goddess Quiz

Whether you respond "Uh huh!" or "That's in the *spirit* of who I am" to a question below, check its box.

❑ Are you a person who is wonderful at organizing fundraisers, peace rallies, political campaigns, and committees, but couldn't microwave even popcorn for love nor money?

❑ Do you tend to notice injustice and suffering that others either ignore or cannot recognize?

❑ When there's a problem, can anyone, even yourself, stop you from trying to fix it?

On to the full quiz:

❑ You write letters to your congressperson, and/or local newspapers, and/or favorite radio talk-show, and/or...

❑ If someone's response to a dilemma is "Well, that's not *my* problem," you're quick to point out that it surely *is*.

❑ You cannot use a single paper towel without hearing a tree fall in the forest.

❑ Your remarkably high ideals and belief that anything is possible are gifts to our society.

❑ And that, people being what they are, is the flip side of a perfection-ism that drives you too hard, and makes you expect too much change too fast, not only of individuals but of society at large.

❑ You have responded to a purely social invitation with "I can't commit to coming because I might get arrested at the demonstration that night." (All joking aside, that was the gist of the email I received from one of my favorite Activist Goddesses, Starhawk, when I invited her to a party. Goddess bless the dedication of the activists!)

❑ Your idea of a sexy mate is someone who rants a lot.

❑ Your other idea of a sexy partner is someone who cannot fathom why you live the way you do. That way, *you* get to be the one who rants.

If you checked off none of the above boxes, not to worry. As long as you vote.

And this might be the time to remind you: these quizzes and descriptions are not the last word. *You* define what makes you an Activist Goddess, Corporate Goddess, etc. So if you donate to Greenpeace, or make prayers for peace, or do *whatever* else as your form of activism, add a description of that to the quiz, put a box next to each of the statements you write, and check off those boxes. Then, even go to the Activist Goddess's chapter and rewrite it!

Don't let anyone tell you that you're in bed with the enemy just because you don't attend rallies. You're grown-up; you can define activism all on your own. I'm making fun of *everyone* and *everything* in this book. Nothing's exempt, even the Goddess types I hold most dear. So, to continue with your Activist Goddess rating, in the spirit of fun:

If you checked off at least two or three, thank you. You're keeping us from going the way of dinosaurs.

Score four to six, and we are indebted as a society. You're a constant aggravation to everyone around you, even other activists, and there is virtue in that.

If seven to eleven descriptions fit you, you haven't had time for sex in months. With your score, you're changing the world like nobody's business, but, girlfriend, you need a break! Take it.

The Goddess-Just-Wants-to-Have-Fun Quiz

Mark the box next to a question you answer with "Yes":

❑ Is laughter one of six things that give your life meaning? The other five being parties, flirting, chocolate, sex, and bright colors.

❑ Do friends ask you to help plan parties and fundraisers because you know exactly what makes—or breaks—an event?

The check-list, if you scored at least one of the above:

❑ The last time you did laundry was, well, *never*! After all, you've got a social life!

❑ There's not a dance you won't try. You've attended classes in everything from Flamenco to hip-hop to ballet. And you don't even mind the discipline of ballet, because the final result is a great time and feeling of freedom when you leap, spin, and expand your spirit.

❑ Folks are surprised and puzzled to discover that you, the original party girl, are a volunteer at the local animal shelter. Your response? "It's fun!"

❑ Your eye for detail is not that good at work. To say the least. The boss doesn't understand why you file everything into the waste-paper basket. But go to a thrilling movie, and you instantaneously memorize every last bit of dialogue, scenery, and costuming.

❑ Yesterday, in the office, you put an important client on hold. The perfectly rational explanation? Your current lover was on the other line!

❑ Once you arrive, whether it's at a party, class, dinner, or work-related situation, things instantly become more light-hearted.

Your rating: If you didn't even check off one of the above boxes, no one is ever going to call you a party girl. (You may, however, be having a great time in your own quiet way.)

If you checked off at least one or two, you've got a zesty love of life, though it's not all-consuming.

If three to five of the boxes are checked, *everyone* will call you a party girl.

Six to eight, and you're dangerously madcap—don't even try to have a serious moment!

The Corporate Goddess Quiz

If your answer to a question below is "Yes" or "The details are wrong, but it's got the *feeling* of who I am," or any variation thereof, check off the box next to the question.

❑ Is your wardrobe, for the most part, divided into three of the following colors: black, navy blue, tan, gray, or white?

❑ Do you, in addition, own one attention-grabbing red suit, for when you want all board members to focus on *you?* (You might also sport khakis and polo shirts, but only on your days off. Oh, and you have a cashmere sweater—I don't know why, you just do.)

Score one or two? You might be a Corporate Goddess. Keep going, checking off any descriptions that fit:

❑ You leave a party after exactly one hour because that is long enough to "show face." Besides, you've got work to do.

❑ Your interest in politics is based on economics.

❑ If family members continue to ask when you're going to settle down and get married (or have children, or …), you're gonna cut them out of your will. And, considering you earn more than all the members of your generation and the past two combined, this is a serious threat!

❑ Your explanation about the best way to reach you is "by cell phone on Mondays. On Tuesdays, it's better to leave me a message on my home phone. That is, if you call before 6 A.M. But if it's urgent, then leave three messages for me: one at work, one on the cell phone, and…oh, forget it! *My schedule is crazy!*"

❑ Coffee, for you, is a sacrament. That, and microwave dinners, posh business luncheons (a chance for some pleasure!), and taking your shoes off when your feet are hidden behind the desk.

❑ Once upon a time you had a social life. You suspect. But it's hard to remember because you haven't had a chance to think about anything except work for three months now!

❑ Someday you're going to meet the right person. Who will own the right suit.

If you scored only one or two of the above items, I've no doubt you're longing for a sugar daddy. I know, because I do dismally on this quiz! But don't forget, ladies—that's not necessarily a bad thing. We all have our strong points.

If you scored three to five, the potential to be a lucrative mover 'n' shaker might exist.

Score six or seven, and I need your advice.

Eight or nine? That's competition for Rupert Murdoch.

The Sex Goddess Quiz

Everyone at one point or another has likely dreamed of being a full-time Sex Goddess.

Only a few get to. Nevertheless, we all can have our triumphantly hot moments. But before you play the Goddess games that can turn anyone into a sexpot, find out how well you're already scoring. Check the box next to any question you answer in the affirmative.

❑ Do you think of sex as wholesome fun?

❑ Is sexuality just a normal part of your everyday life, as opposed to something set apart?

If you answered even one question "yes," move on. Heck, move on anyway. For the fun of it. You're a Sexual Diva if:

❑ The most recent gossip about you is that a married man just sent you roses. The rumor is wrong. It was diamonds.

- ❏ When watching "It's a Wonderful Life," you identify with Violet, town hussy, the most wholesome, innocent charmer imaginable. And, during a flashback, when a child Violet is accused by another girl, "You like *every* boy!" you cry out Violet's response on cue: "What's wrong with *that?*"
- ❏ You understand men. And you enjoy them anyway.
- ❏ Cleavage is not something you ponder when getting dressed. It's a given. Unless you're going for a different look—such as nude!
- ❏ Or your clothing is conservative and modest. But your eyes and/or mouth hold a secret that acts like a magnet.
- ❏ You think of yourself as rather plain, just a natural, sincere woman. People's reactions imply otherwise.
- ❏ Pampering a mate is a total pleasure for you, and whether you do it by giving sensuous massage, or in a way that is not overtly sexy, such as baking your sweetie chocolate chip cookies, you somehow still manage to ignite the fires of passion.
- ❏ You know all the dirty words. You may not *use* them, but you know what they mean.
- ❏ You know that sex is not just a physical act. It's a *very* physical act.

If you only checked one or two boxes—including the mini-quiz—seduction may not be your forte. If so, this will change once you've played the games recommended in the Sex Goddess's chapter.

A score of three to five indicates a healthy number of admirers, some of whom stutter, babble, or blush as soon as you enter the room.

Check off six to nine boxes and you're ready to teach classes on sensuality, sexual confidence, and womanly pride in one's body, whatever its type or shape.

Score perfectly to be Hollywood's next on-screen siren, or, at least, the ideal partner of one very contented lover.

The Out-to-Change-the-World-Goddess Quiz

If you respond "That's me!" to a question, check off the box next to that question. Ready, set, go!

☐ Do you try to explain to friends why they should use Taoist principles for dating?

☐ Are you sometimes puzzled by the amount of praise you receive for helping others, because you assume everyone is just as giving as you?

Score one or two? Then proceed. But you'll grasp the quiz better if you first realize that this deity takes many forms. She may try to change the world through New Age chants, or by working as a fundraiser, or by opening her home to community events. Every Out-to-Change-the-World-Goddess has her own style. But whether a New-Ager, Community Home Goddess, or Ms. Goddess Fundraiser, you're an Out-to-Change-the-World-Goddess if:

☐ When you become sick, you don't ask for help. But you're there in a flash with chicken broth should a friend feel the slightest indication of a cold.

☐ However, if you're a more evolved Out-to-Change-the-World-Goddess, you do request support when you're feeling under the weather. You've learned that you deserve and need the help you so readily provide everyone else. Then, because you've done so much for others, you're not short of people to plump up your pillows, pick up Alka-Seltzer at the drug store, and cook you a meal.

☐ There's a huge pile of papers and books on self-improvement in your home. It's called "your living room." You last saw its floor a year ago when your mother visited and misplaced everything important in a flurry of cleaning up while you were away at work.

❏ Your meditation group (church, coven, synagogue…) has given you a spiritual assignment: to hold silence for one hour a day, and you love it because it's the only breather you have.

❏ Or you love it because you use that hour to plan everything you're going to say the rest of the day in order to fix everyone's problems.

❏ But you worry a bit that your meditation group (church, coven, synagogue…) had an ulterior motive because it was you and only you who was given the hour's silence. You suspect they're all hoping that eventually it'll affect the rest of your day and you'll become quieter during all their planning sessions.

❏ An uncanny eye makes you quick to see any person's problems. Solutions also spring quickly to mind, solutions that are immediate and that anyone can do.

❏ You love arts 'n' crafts, and find them not just decorative but useful. You sell them at fundraisers, wave them over sick friends in healing circles, and/or plaster the town with them to raise consciousness.

❏ The word *busybody* has been used to describe you.

❏ People might also call you *codependent*.

❏ Fortunately, you also hear the words "You've done more for me than you could ever know."

Your rating? Score only one or two out of the above and, sorry, you're completely heartless.

Score three to five, and anybody oriented toward change will be happy to have you as a friend.

Score six to eight, and *anybody* will want your friendship, because you take such good care of everyone around you.

Finally, score nine to twelve and you're likely a fully enlightened being who will not need to incarnate again.

The Trickster Goddess Quiz

If your answer to a question is "Oh, does she have my number!" check off the adjacent box.

❏ Do you have a mischievous streak in you?
❏ Does The Mad Hatter's tea party seem perfectly sensible to you, even spiritual?

Check off one or two of the above and you might qualify. But if you're a Trickster Goddess, you also might find it hard to follow instructions closely enough to *use* this quiz. Nevertheless, a Diva of Disruption often needs to learn discipline, and here's a chance to practice. Check off as many of the items above and below as match you. Of course, being you, you'll come up with a wild and wonderful reason why *nothing* matches you. Despite any protestations you might make, you are a Trickster Goddess if:

❏ You understand that the name *Howard* is innately funny.
❏ You gave that name to your son, dog, cat, guitar, or houseplant.
❏ You might even have given it to all of them!
❏ You're very good at getting people to laugh.
❏ You're not always sure why.
❏ You really do try to be on time. And when you try to explain why you were, nevertheless, late, you take so long that the relevant event is delayed even more.
❏ People who really understand you start smirking when you arrive at an event where pretense reigns.
❏ Leading groups is not for you, because participants follow your lead and nothing gets done.
❏ Repeatedly, you are accused of going on tangents, which always seem

relevant in your own mind.

☐ You will never understand why shocking pink, lime green, and bright orange are not considered fashion neutrals.

Scoring even one or two may mean you're a hopeless fool.

Score three to five, and *please* don't come to my home. (Actually, a huge portion of the people who visit me score high on this quiz. I wonder why.)

Score six to eight and you are divinely disrespectful.

Score nine to twelve and you'll change the world, if you don't destroy it first.

The Bad Girl Goddess Quiz

Make your wicked mark in the box next to any question you answer "Yes."

☐ Do you tend toward black outfits?

☐ Or instead, wear cute pink dresses to disguise your evil soul and thus get away with your destructive, um, I mean helpful, antics?

If you do either of the above, keep going. You qualify as a Bad Girl Goddess if:

☐ You just can't see why people think a little revenge is a *bad* thing.

☐ You believe that if people didn't cut in front of each other in line, all of creation would come undone.

☐ You enjoy religion, and yours is seduction and *Cosmopolitan* magazine.

☐ You use lies like a chef uses spices: a little, a lot, and throughout the day.

☐ You *had* to laugh right in the middle of the wedding, speech, first act, award ceremony, marriage proposal…, I mean, wouldn't anyone?

☐ Finally, your entire existence is predicated on how much you can get away with, not when no one is looking, but when you are in full view!

If you only scored one or two out of the above eight items, stand aside when trouble starts.

If you scored three to five, you've a chance of surviving office politics.

Score six to eight, and people are afraid of you! That is, unless they're scoring high themselves.

The Princess Goddess Quiz

Please, take your feather quill and make your oh-so-royal checkmark next to any question you answer "Yes."

❑ Will you rise before noon only as an experiment in mingling with the masses?

❑ Is stomping your foot rapidly, while exclaiming "no, No, NO!" your idea of making a mild suggestion?

Answer "No" to both of the above questions, and forget exploring your princess status. Answer "Yes" at least once, and you should see how many of the statements below describe you. You may be ready to sashay with the best if:

❑ You couldn't possibly accept a job where you can't wear a tiara.

❑ Once *on* said job, you think wearing the tiara fulfills your job description.

❑ You consider a bed without a canopy one step short of abject deprivation.

❑ Pink is your favorite color *if* it's accented by diamonds.

❑ You feel oh, so faint, so you *couldn't possibly* help out with the dishes (children, typing...).

❑ You speak in sentences in which at least *one* word is "italicized."

Your Princess Goddess analysis: If you only checked off one or two boxes, it's a day to end all your letters by signing off with "Your humble servant." And you had better mean it.

If you scored three to five, I suggest you walk with your head high, because nothing's going to trip you up today.

If you scored six to seven, don't even bother going to work. Spend every hour until nightfall thinking beautiful thoughts.

Finally, if you scored a full eight, the entire world needs your regal inspiration in order to keep on going, so you had better decide which TV and/or radio shows you are willing to grace with an appearance today.

thirteen
modern
goddesses

The Mother Goddess

Are you the Mother Goddess? The Mother Goddess sees that her children get off to school on time. She makes sure they are safe and well fed. She hugs them when they need a hug, and scolds them when they need scolding. And as far as she's concerned, everyone and anyone qualifies as her children—not only her own offspring but her neighbors', as well as the neighbors themselves. And all the dogs and cats in the neighborhood, and the grocers, and gardeners, and teachers. The Mother Goddess may or may not actually *have* biological children.

There are innumerable ways the Mother Goddess might appear. For example, the Earth Mother embodies the wholesomeness of the earth. After all, the Greeks worshiped our planet, and called Her Gaia. The Earth Mother loves to bake, fatten up her mate or friends a bit, and doles out cookies. She tends to wear her hair quite long and listen to songs from the '60s, whether she is old enough to have heard them when they were first released or not. She bakes her own bread, or at least buys it fresh and whole-grain from someone who sports long skirts, peasant blouses, and wavy, abundant locks. This baker may or may not be a gal.

The Mother Goddess might also manifest as the Practical—or *Advice*—Goddess, she who can handle any situation. You can always turn to her for perfect counsel. Her etiquette is flawless because it is based in practicality and goodwill. In fact, Ms. Manners is a *very* Practical Goddess. Interestingly enough, giving advice might be the Practical Goddess's way of bitching about everything that drives her crazy. Is that polite? Somehow she makes it so.

Strengths

Your good points as the Mother Goddess include: selflessness; practicality; and the ability to buckle down and take care of the boring, but necessary, chores that others avoid or forget. You also have endless patience, a sense of humor about life's challenges—both large and small—and an ability to comfort those who suffer, whether the ailment is a scraped knee, lost career, or broken heart. You are the essence of unconditional love; regardless of a person's gender, race, sexual preference, or other factors, you want only the best for them.

Your example teaches all women—and men—what it means to give selflessly.

Weaknesses

Your weaknesses include: too much attention to household details (an inevitable flaw, since it is the flip side of your ability to keep a household running); and ongoing worry about your loved ones. Were you ever to find yourself at a gala cinema premiere, you would probably miss Gwyneth Paltrow's entrance because you were examining the room to determine its level of dust.

You tend never to take time for yourself, and though that's perhaps necessary when, for example, your child is first born, it's become habit with you. Your enormous maternal warmth seems to be matched only by your enormous self-neglect.

Advice for the Mother Goddess

If always putting yourself last is an unnecessary habit, break it! If you don't, you'll just complain all the time, and that alienates people.

Your friends and family *want* you to be happy, which means it's OK to ask them to start doing things for themselves. And if they don't take to it right away, don't nag or decide to go ahead and do it yourself. Give them the time they need to come around on their own. Pushing them will only cause resistance.

Unstinting devotion to those dear to you is your trademark, but it does not always leave you well-rounded. At least once a month, break the mold.

Here are three ways to do that:

1) Spend an hour surfing the Web for something other than recipes.
2) Once the kids are off to school, put on music and dance like a madwoman for five minutes before you start housework.
3) When you get home from work, don't start supper immediately. Instead, eat a piece of chocolate cake with a glass of milk, mothering yourself instead of others for a few minutes.

Never think you're unskilled. The Mother Goddess's homespun abilities make her an excellent businesswoman in many ways. For example, your caring concern, organizational skills, and knack for motivating others to work together as a family are traits employers look for in management position employees.

Besides, the Mother Goddess is not just the mommy—nurturer, baker of cookies, and laundress. She is also the Matriarch—the woman who, instead of being an administrative assistant, is the boss. The woman who, instead of manning the voting booths, has her name on the ballot. Deep down, in every Mother Goddess, exists the Matriarch, and you can call on her whenever you need to. Then, look out, world! Because the Mother Goddess will be running the show, whether it's politics, business, finance, or social change.

Fashion Tips

You may need to add some glamour to your look. You can add sizzle and flash to your hairstyle whether it's long or short. Borrow your six year old daughter's barrettes to create a bit of fun. They'll also prettily get your hair out of your face when you're cooking, hugging, or otherwise fulfilling mom-like duties. Try your *teen* daughter's hair glitter. Splurge on a silk flower to tuck behind your ear or into a bun when you want to look really special.

Other glamour options include: putting on lipstick every day for a week; wearing sexy panties (they take no longer to put on than plain cotton ones, but they make you feel *so* womanly); and splurging on a truly seductive perfume.

You also may need to watch your diet, both in terms of health and weight. A lot of people rely on you, so you need wholesome food. Eating your kiddies' leftovers because you think you're too busy to do otherwise will leave you run down.

If household boredom sets in, either because your mate is neglectful, you hate housework, your pre-kindergartener is not a great conversationalist, or whatever other reason, solve the situation instead of mindlessly eating. If this seems impossible, then find help from someone who will show you otherwise—a friend, sibling, professional, Overeaters Anonymous, whatever. You're worth it. After all, you're the Great Mom!

Games For the Mother Goddess

Reminder: the following not only particularly suit the Mother Goddess, but, like the entire book, should be relevant fun for any woman. The book's games for modern Goddesses are a far cry from anything an ancient deity ever got to do, and show us that risking just a little bit of foolishness by playing a game can change one's life profoundly.

1) "Bless Your Secret Magic Weapon" (see page 125).

2) "Love, Love, and More Love" (see page 134).

3) "How to Be (at Least a Bit of) a Bad Girl Goddess, Version #2" (see page 124), might at first seem an inappropriate choice for the Mother Goddess, because you are so respectable and moral. How could *you* play, with any authority, a game whose nature is not wholly pure and upright? Once you realize that that train of thought designates you as "Goddess Completely Deluded by Thoughts of Grandiosity," you will

also understand that using this game to invoke the Bad Girl Goddess within will actually save your sanity. This game gives Bad Girl Goddess full reign *within*, thus allowing your *external* acts to remain calm, courteous, and reasonable. These latter three traits can be otherwise hard won, yet are especially necessary for mothers.

4) "Cosmic Coincidence Used for Fortune Telling" (see page 130), is ideal for those who, like you, have little time during the day for meditation yet really need some mystical guidance to help them *through* that day.

The Girlfriend Goddess

Are you the Girlfriend Goddess? She is the faithful pal. She's the woman who throws the wedding shower, always helps her best friend clean up after the party, and provides a ready shoulder to cry on. She loves to help and helps to love.

Girlfriend Goddesses tend to be collectors. They collect recipes, so that they can bring the best dishes to their friends' parties. They clip out coupons for items that their friends need. They gather wisdom to distribute freely to those they love. Needless to say, they also collect friends—everyone wants to sign up!

Strengths

There is no situation you can't handle, as long as you are doing so to help out a pal. You seem to understand your friends' problems, needs, and hopes better than they do themselves. So you're always there with ideal sympathy and the wisdom to do exactly what they need you to do.

Your resourcefulness is an asset not only to your friends but also to your family and employer. You've a creative approach to problem solving that others value.

Your insight into others is remarkable, even though you may not yet be able to apply this wisdom for your own needs. In other words, you see deeply into everyone's hearts and souls, but when you try to do this in a situation that affects only you, you don't analyze well. But you do have the potential to use your analytical abilities for your own well-being, if you work at it. In the meantime, consider yourself lucky that you are able to help others figure out what's what in *their* lives.

I suspect Girlfriend Goddess's depth of perception often extends to an excellent intuition or other psychic ability. A Girlfriend Goddess once hired me to do psychic readings at a party. After listening in for a while, she "set up shop" next to me. She became more and more excited as we did readings side by side, until she was grinning like a kid with a cute new pink dress. She had realized that, without any previous experience as a reader, she could right then and there do what I was doing. I loved it! Anyone she read for said her insights were spot on! She was a natural.

But this is not actually that surprising. I think it may be pretty typical of Girlfriend Goddesses. Besides, all we Goddesses have some degree of psychic ability, in one form or another, whether it's intuition, hunches, empathy, or any of the other innumerable possibilities. It might be repressed or need developing, but it's there.

At the end of your life, Ms. Girlfriend Goddess, you'll be able to measure your success by all the help, love, and kindness you extended.

Weaknesses

Confidence is not your strong trait. You tend to feel your looks are not the best, when in fact you might be absolutely stunning! When it comes to looking for a mate, you are too often tempted to settle for second best.

You need more of a life of your own. The generosity you show is authentic and worthy of applause, but sometimes it swallows up your whole life.

Occasionally, self-pity envelops you. Everyone seems too busy to give you the love, sympathy, and aid you so readily provide to others. Friends seem to have forgotten you exist. Until, yup—there's the phone ringing—someone *needs* something.

Feeling sorry for yourself isn't necessarily the worst of it. Eventually, you might start harboring resentments that you give all the help and they (whoever *they* are) have all the fun. But no one's perfect, so read on for solutions regarding your shortcomings.

Guidance for Godlike Girlfriends

Enter into a helping profession such as counseling. Earning money for your caring acts can resolve your sense of no payback.

Try going out for no other reason than to have a good time. If resentment about others' getting to do so is getting to you, maybe it's because you haven't learned to play yourself. Go skydiving. Take a class in salsa dancing.

Call up a friend and ask her or him to go along. But, for heaven's sake, be light-hearted when you make your request. Maybe people forget to call you when there's a party on because your steadfast seriousness, which is ideal when needed, is not balanced by enough simple, easy-going frivolity. Practice enjoying things just for the sake of pleasure. If there's no one to join you, gallivant about on your own, teaching yourself how to have a good time. Eventually, your smile will become bigger, your step more relaxed and confident, your life more full. And that will make people call you up for dates, parties, and the like. Learning a new dance or taking on a hobby will also improve your self-image; you'll feel more assured and poised.

If, like my client Katya, you can't get a life of your own no matter how hard you try, and it's really bothering you, get help. Talk about it with a friend or your mom. (Remember, Mom can also be the Advice Goddess!) Maybe see a therapist or spiritual counselor. As the latter, I was able to help Katya not only see why she lived too much for others but also help her change that. And while we were at it, we discovered her inner blocks to romance and what to do about them. She's happily married now.

Meditation and other spiritual practices suit you. You might even find yourself teaching them. But they do well by you for your own sake, helping you focus on finding yourself instead of just finding dates for your girlfriends.

Don't be afraid to flirt with the most handsome, desirable, sexy creature you meet. If nothing else, it's good practice. And you also might discover that you are a catch yourself! You are very likely date bait!

In the section on your strengths I mentioned Girlfriend Goddesses' inability to analyze their own situations. In the case of the Girlfriend Goddess at the party, she was so excited about her psychic ability that she studied with me to cultivate it further. As her natural gift bloomed, she discovered a by-product: she was also able to analyze her own life as well as she did other people's.

That might seem an inexplicable result, especially since I am not talking about a *psychic* ability to analyze her own life. But if one does anything to feel more secure in *any* type of perception, whether psychic or totally left-brain, one feels more confident overall. Also, removing blocks to one type of perception often unblocks others. If, for example, you learn to read psychically, you trust your common sense more. And vice versa. So my advice is that you work on improving any mode of perception, whether psychic ability or non-psychic perception such as would be enhanced by studying philosophy or math; or just learn to listen to your own common sense more often when it comes to your own life instead of only when it comes to others'.

Last of all, honor yourself for the kind, down-to-earth, giving woman you are. People are lucky to have you in their lives.

Fashion Tips

If anyone is oblivious of how to adorn herself, it's you. So you may want to get a fashion analysis. If you can't afford to have it done professionally, here's what I've done in the past, and it's really helped me learn what works on me:

I enlist the sales clerk in the clothing store when I'm not sure about fit. She or he can be a great help.

I've asked a friend to help me shop for a particular occasion. She'll tell me what's suitable, and likely talk me into wearing something much more flattering than what I would have picked out on my own.

I also briefly joined an online women's fashion list. There, I learned how to dress best for my build, what colors suit me, and so on. It was a fab, free way to pick up fashion sense.

Games for the Girlfriend Goddess

1) "Presto! Instant Sex Magic!" (see page 117) is dedicated to Sex Goddess par excellent, Marilyn Monroe, and would leave her jealous because it so enhances its participants' sexual glamour. Use this game to get a life of your own!

2) "Princess Pink Day" (see page 126) is perfect self-indulgence for anyone like you, whose life tends to, well, not exist! Kidding aside—because you *do* have a good life, you just don't focus enough of it on yourself—this game provides balance to your selflessness. It also lifts your spirits so that you can keep on being the giving person you love to be.

   If one wants to be more of a Girlfriend Goddess, lead a Princess Pink Day for your friends. This will help nurture your giving traits.

3) "Cosmic Coincidence Used For Fortune Telling" (see page 130) might help you find mystical guidance, whether you need to figure out how

to be a really good Girlfriend Goddess, or if you already are one, how you can get out of wearing that awful bridesmaid's dress.

4) "Bless Your Secret Magic Weapon" (see page 125) inspires self-confidence, or whatever other trait you think you might need.

The Goddess of Love

The Goddess of Love! The Goddess of Love rules over all forms of love: love of one's family or job, love of mother earth, love of justice, and, of course, glance-meets-glance-ooh-la-la love! Choose your own variation—this is love we're talking about!

Strengths

The Goddess of Love is kind, attractive (whether she's even pretty by current standards or not), patient, and good with all kinds of people. She listens when people talk and seems to really understand the core issues they're addressing. She doesn't bat an eyelash when trouble appears because, deep in her heart, she knows love conquers all. Always willing to stand up for the underdog, this woman is an opponent that would make any bullying politician quake—because love cannot be conquered!

The Goddess of Love often has a strong spiritual side, even if she is not religious. She may not even see herself as spiritual, and she definitely won't preach at people, but her whole life embodies spirituality. She teaches, often unconsciously, by example.

Weaknesses

She *does* have them, though that might seem hard to believe. She can become a bit too proud, because all her goodness and care for others can make her think she walks on water. She can also be a bit too starry-eyed; sometimes a harsh justice is needed, and she doesn't have the heart for that.

The shirt off her back is yours for the asking, but she might forget that it won't fit you. In other words, she's not always practical in her efforts to help others.

The Goddess of Love has a hard time choosing the right mate. She loves *all* her suitors and they all seem special.

Sometimes, focus is hard for her. She sees so much need, feels love for so many people, and has such a dreamy way of looking at things that she cannot always follow through on her good-natured impulses.

Helpful Hints for the Goddess of Love

If Goddess of Love describes you, then, my dear, take a course in math, history, or any other topic that'll ground you better into the realities of life. But don't get *too* so-called realistic: your greatest strength is your enduring belief in goodness and love.

Your dream partner is probably your opposite. Totally down-to-earth, logical instead of emotional, and maybe even a bit cynical. Don't try to change that cynic into a dreamer. Just be loving, and your kindness might eventually cause a thaw. Trying to force a change only makes people dig in their heels.

If you ever become frustrated because your family (friends, neighbors, coworkers) insist your high values are naive, agree that you're a bit too optimistic—because *that* much is true and saying so will keep the peace. But stay true to your beliefs, because everyone needs you to do so, and, deep down, they probably know it.

You can't work just any job, so choose carefully. Your best career choices include: social worker; stay-at-home Mom; waitress; restaurant owner; nurse; hospice worker; teacher of young children. And whether you pursue the following activities professionally or not, they suit you: spiritual counseling; grass roots activism; political lobbying; religious leadership.

Fashion Tips

Your dreamy personality lets you wear soft, flowing clothes. Even if you are a big woman, you can get away with it. If you don't think so, you may want to talk to an fashion expert. Fit, and knowing how to dress for your particular build, is everything. You can be six feet tall, fabulously muscled like a long, lean basketball player, and still look loveable in pink.

Try something dramatic and romantic with your hair. You may want to let it grow long—natural locks to the shoulders, or maybe even to your waist, are fab! And when you need your hair out of the way, you can arrange a bun so that locks and wisps fall down instead of the bun looking perfect, strict, and tight. Cute. If you prefer short hair, try for something natural and soft.

Games for the Love Goddess

1) "Love, Love, and More Love" (see page 134).
2) As good as you are, you need to play "How to Be (at Least a Bit of) a Bad Girl Goddess, Version #1" to get some balance (see page 122).
3) "The Big Secret" (see page 121) might at first seem an odd game of choice for someone who is, or wants to be, a Love Goddess. But the game helps bolster the serenity needed to face any situation with aplomb. Grace and kindness under fire *define* the Goddess of Love.

The Activist Goddess

The Activist Goddess! She loves nature, lives to help others, and is willing to forsake leisure time in a bubble bath for a long night of stuffing envelopes or writing strategies on how to help the world embrace diversity.

Strengths

Vitality, enthusiasm, and optimism are never lacking, nor are concern and compassion for the underdogs of our world. You tend to be coura-geous. No matter how afraid you are, you do the right thing. Leadership comes easily to you, as does the ability to inspire others to great acts.

Weaknesses

Your remarkable, commendable, and endless compassion for humanity as a whole can disappear when you are faced with an individual. In other words, you are so focused on the big picture that you can forget to be con-siderate to those who are fighting the good fight with you.

You also might lose compassion for people whose political ideals and goals are different from your own. It's wonderful that you fight for what you believe in. But others have that same right and need to follow their own truths.

Not that I expect you to be a perfect saint—Goddesses and saints are dif-ferent creatures. Yes! So I am not suggesting you justify *any* opponent's foolish, outrageous, or inhumane decisions. But watch that, in the heat of things, you don't unconsciously sink to the level of your adversary if they're being cruel or otherwise inappropriate. Because then *you* become the problem, perpetrating the very wrongs you oppose. The danger here is becoming that which you battle. Compassion is the safeguard.

When others ignore politics altogether and focus on the needs of their families and mainstream job, you can be, well, a real snob about it. Worse, you might even verbally attack, erroneously thinking unkind words can change their priorities. Maybe their priorities are fine.

My friend, Stephanie Fay, is not political, but she lovingly supports her friends who are. She wisely says to them, "While you guys are all battling it out, some of us have to keep the gears rolling so that there's something *here* when the battle's over." Wise woman! So, remember, each person is a Goddess, tending to her piece of the work.

Besides, political activists are not the only responsible citizens trying to change things. The Out-to-Change-the-World-Goddess, for example, makes a difference in a more personal way, such as by reading stories to children in a homeless shelter or informally counseling friend after friend.

Then there are women who improve things for everyone by quietly going about their own business. Perhaps they are Mother Goddesses, raising children with high morals. Or are Goddesses of Love who do their job in a supermarket with such sweet cheer and kindness it starts ripples of goodwill that spread for miles.

Another problem you might have is impatience, a trait that can defeat you. Anger might also be an issue. Social change is almost always slow to happen, which can make one feel crazy. The suffering that goes on because of our species' endlessly dragging feet is bound to make *anyone* nuts! But, fact is, when you lose your innate tactfulness, you defeat your own purpose. Your healthy anger and distress at injustice, hunger, war atrocities, and other inhumanities are good things. They motivate you. But when they get the better of you, you become dismally ineffective. I suspect that, since you are on the front lines, it is inevitable that sometimes your pain and/or anger overwhelms you. Anyone doing their best—whether mother, CEO, or activist—is on the front lines of life and can become overwhelmed. But do what you can. Suggestions are below.

Guidance for the Rabble-Rousing Goddess

Never let go of your ideals and optimism. But practice acceptance of your own limits so that you don't overwork yourself into an illness or wake up one day to realize you have no social life, lover, or other non-work satisfaction. Overwork leaves you frazzled. That's when your temper is more likely to flare.

Practice patience with others: the perfect ideal is unattainable; motivate folks to work *toward* it, but love them despite their failings.

Since you tend to feel you are the only one trying so hard and sacrificing so much, consider this: Most of the Goddess types give too much, rest too little, and need more support. Many women can agree on this issue, so maybe it's a meeting point, a common problem around which you can find sisterhood with other women instead of feeling sorry for yourself or all-that-pompously-noble. Perhaps, instead of feeling all alone, you can find much-needed support by getting together with other women—whether they're activists or not. Maybe you and they can teach each other what lessons you have all learned about self-care and about tending to one's own needs, not just to those of other people. Maybe this sort of dialogue is a way to transcend your differences with other women instead of judging them for those differences.

Okay. I just realized that what I thought was new thinking is a '60s feminist rap.

But I mean it, anyway. On to more helpful hints for the Activist Goddess:

Do you feel guilty, or otherwise uncomfortable, if you try to love and respect yourself as the Goddess you are? Activists often hold humankind precious, but lack the same feelings for themselves. If you have this problem, use the bubble bath in the Mother Goddess chapter. And as you soak, try to pinpoint what's inside you that is causing the discomfort. Is it nagging guilt telling you that your human failings make you unworthy of self-respect? Or fear that someone will think you're a snob if you hold your head high? Or concern that friends will laugh if you try something new? Whatever the inner block, pretend that it's being washed away in the bath. This sort of act feeds a message to your whole being, even your unconscious mind, that you can let go of the block. By the way, this Goddess Bath Ceremony is good for *any* type of Goddess who needs a boost.

Honor your anger about the wrongs of the world. Your anger is a sacred fire that blazes in the darkness, shedding light on cruelty, and making it more difficult for people to ignore wrongdoing. We all realize that if you suppress your anger, it doesn't go away. It just lurks deep inside you, controlling you unconsciously. Tucked away like that, it is not available as emotional fuel to drive you toward important change.

But don't let your anger get the better of you. As soon as you lose your temper, people can avoid looking at the real problems and instead focus on your lack of control. You want to learn a balance between expressing and using your anger, and letting it use you. If you don't have tools to do this, find them. Ask colleagues. Read up. Learn them in a counseling session (see "Modern Resources for Modern Goddesses," page 143). If none of these means suit, find another!

Become able to share responsibility. You don't have to do everything yourself.

Every single day, applaud yourself for being an Activist Goddess. In one day, you do far more for the betterment of humankind as a whole than most people are in a position to do in a lifetime.

Fashion Tips

Wear clothes you don't mind getting dirty if you do sit-ins.

Don outfits that make you look like a lawyer when you're speaking in front of a city council.

Try black in the middle of the night when you're spray-painting slogans on billboards.

And the rest of the time, dress however you want. You deserve it!

As a matter of fact, see that you hang a couple of items in your closet that make you feel special. Whether it's a Ren Faire costume, a sexy red negligee, or a *Breakfast at Tiffany's* little black dress with pearls, have a few outfits that are totally the secret, private you.

Games for the Activist Goddess

1) "Love, Love, and More Love" (see page 134) is the essence of the Activist Goddess. Of course, you might say you have no time for games, because you are out trying to save the world. You need to make the time! Games are one way to maintain the balance you, and we all, require.

2) "Princess Pink Day" (see page 126) also provides balance to your life, even if you only play it for an hour instead of a full day.

3) "The 'I Can't Hear You' Game" (see page 119) helps you bolster the high energy, courage, and sass needed to plunge into life's battles, political and otherwise.

Goddess-Just-Wants-to-Have-Fun

This Goddess loves new crazes, dances her way through party after party, and was last seen in the company of the most charming young man. Or was that charming young *men*? My, my!

Strengths

Well, obviously, you're fun! But you are also charming, and you laugh delightedly at anyone's jokes—even if they're not that funny—which makes you a big ego boost to those around you.

It's never boring being with you, and, since you're adventurous, you're always willing to go along with a friend's lunatic schemes instead of acting like a wet blanket.

Life, strangely enough, feels more meaningful in your presence. You invest whatever you do with enthusiasm and razzle-dazzle, so that anything and everything becomes bigger than life.

You've a great sense of humor and can crack a joke with the best of them. If ever there were a person who knew how to throw a pajama party, you're her. You can spin a ghost story 'til your own hair stands on end; pick the perfect video to watch at 2 A.M.; choose the ideal nail color for everyone's manicure; and concoct the gooiest, most calorie-filled food a group of women in pj's ever consumed.

You teach us all how to be more light-hearted, instead of becoming bogged down by daily upsets, or endlessly dwelling on problems. You know instinctively that when one forgets to play, problems start to loom heavier and heavier, and even appear unsolvable. When someone needs a fresh perspective, she can go play with you until it clears her mind and she can think straight again. Then she's ready to tackle her issue.

Weaknesses

Your flaws are obvious. Luckily, a dazzling personality lets you get away with them. Some of the time. But deep down (and maybe even right there at a conscious level) people's less desirable traits hurt them. So watch out for the following: forgetfulness about responsibilities when something more entertaining comes along; too speedy an attempt to cheer up a troubled friend when a more serious approach is needed, such as listening solemnly to a tale of woe or drying someone's tears; an occasional lapse of only looking at the surface instead of at the less apparent but more enduring values.

Guidance for the Giddily Divine You

You have a remarkable ability to distract people from even the most serious problems, providing them with a moment's respite and a chance to have their spirits lifted. Just know when this is the right action, and when you instead need to calm down, sober up, and become serious. Otherwise, friends may be hurt, feeling you're making light of their problems.

Your dream mate? Someone who can keep up with you! And who is willing to try the new and wild activities you're always suggesting.

Choose your career carefully. Either hold a job that gives you the money and freedom to focus fully on your recreation time, or have a career that is a blast! How about being a party planner? Your enthusiasm and dazzle make you a natural candidate for work as an agent or publicist for entertainers or authors. The hard work could be too demanding for you, but, on the other hand, the media world is exciting and adrenaline-driven, and that's like manna from heaven for you.

Fashion Tips

Ideal fashions for you are, of course, trendy, colorful, and exciting. But make sure you choose what truly suits your build, coloring, and activities. Don't look foolish just because an item of clothing was seen in *Vogue* last week. Don't buy pencil-slim full-length skirts when you're a wild dancer, love to run along the beach, and play kickball three times a week. Part of what makes you so appealing is your own quirkiness. So dress to highlight your best traits; within the wide range of the latest fashions, there's plenty to choose from.

Games for Goddess-Just-Wants-to-Have-Fun

There's no game that's *not* on the list of Goddess-Just-Wants-to-Have-Fun. (GJWTHF, for short.) She leads them all well and enjoys each and every one. But if you need to be more GJWTHF yourself—and there's rarely a Goddess who doesn't need to be more GJWTHF, except, of course, GJWTHF—try the following:

1) "Princess Pink Day" (see page 126).
2) "Cosmic Coincidental Fortune Telling Stories" (see page 131).
3) "Bless Your Secret Magic Weapon" (see page 125).

Corporate Goddess

Are you a Corporate Goddess? The Corporate Goddess has it made when it comes to business and investments. She is independent, loves her work, and might be looking for that one special someone who is her equal and who wants to build a life with a powerful, brilliant woman. The word *cute* is not in her vocabulary—unless she writes promotional copy.

Strengths

The Corporate Goddess understands the business world through and through, a realm that, at least to some degree, confuses many other women. She works hard to stand on her own two feet instead of waiting for someone else to take care of her. Her organizational skills, management abilities, and overall savvy make her someone you want on your team. She understands responsibility, deadlines, and priorities—so you can always count on her.

Her fashion sense is impeccable, as is her hair and overall grooming. She sees that each detail is perfect.

Weaknesses

The Corporate Goddess overworks then wonders why life is not fulfilling. Well-rounded is *not* the word to describe her. Sometimes, she neglects not only her own emotional needs, but those of her friends. And she is prone to forget that the true bottom line is not the dollar. Her impatience is legendary; it's still a man's world in a lot of ways, and her fight in it can make her testy. For one thing, her frustration may be easily aroused with other women. She forgets that we're all in this together.

Dispensation of Divine Direction

If you're a Corporate Goddess, try to be more balanced. I know you feel like there's not enough time to achieve your career goals *and* have a personal life, but if you don't start living fully now, you never will. Because there will *always* be a reason that work has to come first, and you just have to say "No" to that, or it will never change.

Learn to stop several times a day and take deep breaths. I'd like to say this will help you stay calm, patient with others, and clear-headed. Fact is, it *might* do so. But, unfortunately, there's an even more pressing reason I suggest it. Adrenaline-driven thought and action seem to be your default modes of operation. You don't pause for a second. Taking a few breaths might at least remind you *to* breathe! Women as busy as you tend to hold their breath.

As to being more patient, calm, and clearheaded: try a meditation practice. It can make all the difference. Or at least remind you to breathe.

Finally, admire yourself as much as you can. Despite the feminist movement, you still receive a lot of negative input for being so career oriented. So, give yourself as much praise and reward as you can. You're paving the way for all of us.

Fashion Tips

Buy one outrageous, foolishly feminine or otherwise frivolous outfit. If that idea does not appeal to you, I suggest you at least window shop for one and maybe even try a few items on. It might surprise you. For example, such an outfit, or even window shopping for one, might give you a breather from your usual seriousness or light up the hidden part of you (hidden, perhaps, even from yourself) that needs to be a bit silly, or mischievous, or otherwise not so businesslike.

All professional women somehow seem to know the secret of red lipstick: wearing it frightens people one is competing with. So, when you go on a date, in order to lay down your battle mentality, wear pink lip-color. Romance is not a business negotiation, no matter who tells you otherwise.

Games for the Corporate Goddess

1) "The Big Secret" (see page 121) is a game whereby a Goddess can blithely deal with bosses, neighbors, competitors, and others who are annoying. The secret? To pretend you have one! Smugly. While keeping that smugness a delicious part of the secret as well!

2) "The 'I Can't Hear You' Game" (see page 119) helps you go to work fully defended against negative input. You may also want to play it before visiting parents who insist you be more traditionally female. It'll help you stay serene.

3) "Bless Your Secret Magic Weapon" (see page 125) is ideal, not only generally speaking for you, but also as a way to feel even *more* powerful when you wear that red lipstick.

4) "How to Be (at Least a Bit of) a Bad Girl Goddess, Version #2" (see page 124) will help you gain not only the "bad" you need, but give you—or any woman—yet another way to climb the corporate ladder blithely.

Sex Goddess

Are you a Sex Goddess? A Sex Goddess thinks slinky black negligees are a must, and she may actually have read the *Kama Sutra*. There is also another type of Sex Goddess: this version may wear cotton undies and never have looked at a *Playgirl*, but she knows what she likes, and she goes after it!

In fact, there are many types of Sex Goddess. After all, sex is very personal, and we each have our own way of enjoying our bodies and sexual relationships. It's not enough to know whether you're a Sex Goddess because when you know which *type* of Sex Goddess you are, you can give it freer expression. Also, you'll better understand your strong and weak points and how to apply the helpful hints below. Finally, whatever type of Goddess you are: when trying to understand and support the other women in your life, it helps to know what type of Sex Goddess a given woman might be. Below are a few of the innumerable possible Sex Goddesses—if you don't find your own particular type, read on, and you'll find ideas about honoring the Sex Goddess *you* are!

First, let's look at the Warm Fuzzy Sex Goddess. She's an enigma to her friends. She bakes—she is in fact thoroughly domestic—and she would blush if you so much as said the word *orgasm,* but your male buddies fall all over her. Her secret? Well, it's a few things. First of all, it's not that she's a prude. Her embarrassment at blatant sexual announcements or acts is actually rooted in an extremely passionate personality. She's one of the most sexual creatures on this planet. And therefore she likes a sense of privacy. Her enormous capacity for pleasures of the flesh doesn't shame her, mind you. She just wants the safe haven of one partner—this type of Goddess tends toward monogamy—so that she feels secure when she goes for broke. She has the sort of passion that is so all-consuming and totally giving that it leaves her far too vulnerable for her to refer to it casually. She keeps sex in a very special place. And that discretion is like honey to the bee.

Her other secret is that she honors sexuality. She knows it's healthy and that pure physical pleasure is sacred as long as it hurts no one. Her seeming prudery on the street changes into ribald, unrestrained, and unashamed hedonism in the bedroom. And, somehow, when a person is looking for a lover, they can sense this about the Warm Fuzzy Sex Goddess.

Next, there's the Professional Sex Goddess, who ranges from the movie star to the fashion model to the sex-industry worker. And lest you sit up in a huff over the latter, consider this: it is a terrible thing when financial hardship forces a woman to lower herself by taking a demeaning job. The sex industry has spared many women this fate, saving them from, for example, office work. (More later about understanding this deity who gives *currency* a bit of a different meaning.)

Then, there's the Glamour Sex Goddess: She is very flashy, but don't be deceived. All that glitter draws the fellows, who then discover a sweet, down-home girl under the rhinestones, Wonderbra, and hot-pink capris. Lots of glamour and lots of heart.

Finally, let's look at the Celibate Sex Goddess, who only *seems* a contradiction in terms. A woman cannot be fully sexual unless she is in complete control of her body. That includes the option of engaging in no sexual activity, whether for a night or for a year. Women do not lose their sexuality when they say "No."

For example, a while back a woman came to me for counseling because she had had several unhappy affairs and wanted to change that pattern. I guide people by using my intuition—some people call it psychic ability—and, in her case, the solution that came to me was for her to swear off relationships for a bit.

During that respite, we did a few more sessions to help her learn to use her solitude for self-discovery. We also used those sessions to discuss her modus operandi. What we learned together is best expressed by her:

"Not getting sexual with anyone for a while highlighted drastically what I want and don't want, what behavior makes me happy and what doesn't. I was doing a lot of things that made me miserable and have found other behavior.

"I even realized that the men I dated were all great guys, so I am not saying anything against any of them. I am saying that I was able to see my *own* shortcomings and errors very clearly by taking a break.

"I feel like I'm fully alive sexually now, because I know who I am, as well as what I was doing wrong. I still want an involvement, but time's given me new patience and self-respect. So I'm ready to date again and do it right this time."

Sexuality exists in a woman whether she is celibate or not. It is part of her being. Even if it is suppressed, or channeled into something else, it is part of each of us.

Any woman who truly claims her sexuality is a Sex Goddess. Even if she claims it through celibacy.

Now, let's reveal a very special Sex Goddess who may or may not be indicated in the Sex Goddess quiz. Is there another type of Sex Goddess that *you* are? Then write down a trait or several that make you think so. And *voila!* You've created a new Goddess, one who's actually been there all along, needing to be worshipped by you—that's self-love—and by all you meet! Name the unique Sex Goddess that *you* are.

Understanding one's uniqueness, whether as a Sex Goddess or anything else—artist, mother, store clerk—means not limiting or pigeonholing your view of yourself. For example, I'm a bit Warm Fuzzy Sex Goddess yet a bit like Violet in *It's a Wonderful Life*, who was mentioned in the Sex Goddess quiz. I'm like the latter in that I'm an outrageous flirt. But I'm all talk, and in actuality very private about sex. Go figure! It makes me comfortable with my sexuality to let that contradiction be, because it makes *gut* sense to me.

So when you list the special traits that make *you* a Sex Goddess, don't judge their validity or ponder their sensual merit too much. Remember, this is supposed to be fun! Just sit down, alone or with friends, and do it off-the-cuff. Spontaneous listing may cut to the truth more than anything you think out carefully.

Of course, some women who feel less secure in, or even terrible about, their sexuality can't do this exercise in a fun, easy-going way. In that case, ask a friend to make the list for you.

If you're too private for that, and really want to know what makes *you* a Sex Goddess, go ahead and take your time. Look through your wardrobe to see what's striking and eye-catching. Ask yourself if there are any foods in which you take sensual delight. Are there special erotic spots on your body? Sexy compliments you've received?

If none of my suggestions are relevant, that doesn't mean you're dowdy and sexless. I can only mention a few of the limitless possibilities. And sexuality is a *very* individual thing.

Determining what you as a unique person find sexy in yourself might mean taking a leap of faith—faith in your own opinion. Yes, this is not the way we usually think of *leap of faith*. But trust in oneself and in a Supreme Being are not diametrically opposed. Actually, for some people faith in God(dess)'s beneficence allows them faith in their own opinion. You might want to pray for trust in yourself. Sorry, I had to have my minister moment. But honor your own idea of sexiness, even if you don't understand it or have never heard of anything like it. Honor it even if it's a tiny glimmer of an idea; think of it as a place to start. And if you change your mind—let's say you get off to a false start—you've perhaps taken that first tiny step that starts all fruitful journeys. As long as your sexuality hurts no one, it's yours, free to be whatever it is.

Whether it's believing in yourself, letting go of guilt, or doing the hula, do what it takes to live the life you want, sexually or otherwise. Dare to be a Goddess! The following story might encourage you:

I teach tele-seminars—classes by phone—and one is about sacred sexuality. Sacred sexuality embraces the earthy spirituality of sex and embodies the belief that the material world, as a gift from our Creator, is meant to be enjoyed.

In one class, a woman confessed that she had never felt desirable, and, in fact, didn't have much interest in sex anyway. If someone has no desire for sex, and is happy with that, I support them. But she cried, sobbing quietly, as she explained that she knew she was missing something and desperately wanted to experience the special connection to someone she knew sex could bring.

She said, "I have never told anyone this before. Everyone always thinks I'm so independent that I'm afraid to say anything. My friends think it's great that I focus on my job, take good care of my mother, and don't worry about the rest like they do. But I'm lonely. And I don't know what to do."

We got down to business. The first step was a psychic reading—that's how I do my counseling—to determine what was blocking her. I saw unacknowledged grief and anger she didn't know how to handle.

After helping her feel the buried sorrow she was carrying, I gave her a Native American grieving rite to do with the support of her friends.

I also told her, guided again by my intuition, "Your anger is unmanageable because as a child you were repeatedly told 'Stop being such a bother!' or 'Why are you so demanding?' Your perfectly legitimate childhood needs were neither met nor validated. This has made you think that your anger at this neglect is also invalid, so you suppressed the anger, and it surfaces only as tantrums."

Once she confirmed my reading was correct, she was able to allow her anger at past and present wrongs to come out more naturally and less harmfully.

Grief and anger somewhat healed, she was able to start to view her sexual needs as valid. I told her to create a Sex Goddess costume for herself. She shopped for weeks, at first tentatively, still unsure about her self as a sexual being. But with the support of the rest of the class, she finally adorned herself as her sensual ideal.

It took more than that, however, for her to fully claim her sexuality. We had to work through more issues first, for example, her fear that self-expression, sexual or otherwise, would meet with disapproval. Also, her anger needed more work before she could feel it was a healthy emotion and actually an asset.

But bit by bit, we were able to break through her inner blocks to sensuality and spontaneity. It took time, but she now knows she's a Sex Goddess and is enjoying the benefits thereof.

My point? Whether it's because of your sexuality or something else, if you're not happy, change that. Lose weight. Leave your job. Take yoga classes. Try to row across the English Channel. It doesn't matter if it takes time; it's worth it. Often the first step in solving a problem is to do what my student did—tell someone! Her second step was to get help. We Goddesses can be too independent sometimes. Or too proud. Or too frightened to seek support.

Whether you seek professional help or that of a friend or parent, you are being a Goddess! Myth tells us that when the ancient deities got into trouble, they sat down with each other and problem-solved. I'm spending a little extra time problem-solving with you in this chapter, because, as was the case with ancient Goddesses, sex and romance can cause a lot of trouble for us modern gals.

I would be remiss if I did not add that if you don't want to be a Sex Goddess, that's good, too! Heck, think of all the money you'll save never buying a Wonderbra. And you'll have lots of time for changing the world, as well as changing your hairstyle, eating popcorn, making chocolate-chip cookies, and traveling in Europe. Be the Goddess *you* are.

But if you are a Sex Goddess:

Strengths

If you're a Sex Goddess, you're sexy. And then you're sexy. Then you're sexy again. I'm joking, but it's also true—this is a strong asset. Some women would give just about anything to have the sexiness you display just by raising your little finger.

You can blink and the waiter dashes to your table. Even if he's gay—he wants to be up close to study your makeup. (As if *eyeliner* is what makes you fabulous.)

You're a free spirit and tend to not judge others. Passion is not a bad word to you.

You often are a Love Goddess as well. I mean, your heart is big, you'll share your home, your clothes, your money, with anyone in need.

Perhaps because people so easily misunderstand you, you show sympathy for rebels and outcasts. You may not know what advice to give, but you're a good listener. Your unconditional warmth is thoroughly maternal—when someone comes to you upset, they discover a true Mother Goddess in you.

Despite the belief that one is either a "Madonna or a whore," perhaps some of your sexiness comes from a combination of the two. Sheer mother love is sexy, even if folks don't know that *that* is what's turning them on.

Weaknesses

Sometimes, Sex Goddesses forget they have value outside the bedroom. Marilyn Monroe was a brilliant woman. Her comedic roles displayed consummate timing. Whether singing, dancing, or acting, there wasn't a thoughtless, random gesture or sound in her work.

A Sex Goddess might try to coast on her allure. And it'll work. But not all the time. Then she is prone to become resentful and pretend to herself she doesn't understand what happened.

Though on some level everyone adores a Sex Goddess, people often fear her as well, because this society teaches us to be afraid of sex and passion. Sometimes Sex Goddesses buy into this cultural bias and feel bad about themselves instead of realizing that they might be able to model healthy attitudes about bodies, sensuality, and freedom of expression. They might lose their self-esteem, influenced by a friend or suitor who is both tantalized and repulsed.

A Sex Goddess might also start dishonoring sex herself by focusing too much on it and forgetting there are other things to life.

Tips to the Titillating

Well, I hesitate to give you, the Sex Goddess, advice. Mostly because I'm dying to hear *yours*. But here goes.

Love yourself. Everyone else *worships* you, in the sense of placing you on a pedestal, of being enamored of you, and charmed by your magic, but it's of no value unless you love yourself as well as you possibly can.

Give all the advice you can to girlfriends. Yes, I'm saying this because I want to hear your secrets. But, more, it's because *you* need the benefits of female bonding. Your popularity can make other women jealous, and without friends life eventually becomes sad. So share your sexual wisdom and do anything else possible to cultivate girlfriends.

Enjoy your life. Sexuality is God(dess) given, a natural part of us, meant to be celebrated. Aren't you lucky to be such a turn-on? Yes! If anyone tells you different, don't be alone with your sadness. Talk it over, and don't let the taboos on sexuality make you hush up.

Know your value is not just sexual. No person is as one-dimensional as that.

The ancient text called the *Kama Sutra* taught courtesans to be amazingly well-rounded. Performance arts, ability with crafts, knowledge of ointments, ability to converse about politics, flower arranging—these are just a few of the many skills the great courtesans of the world have excelled in. It is part of what makes them great.

Fashion Tips

Don't feel you have to give up sexy clothing as you grow older. We change as we move through life's passages, so if you truly want to dress down, that's fine. But you don't have to. There are plenty of "old maids" around having happy flings in their razzle-dazzle outfits!

Sure, we get rounder as the years roll by. But some people find that hot. You just may have to find a *different* sexy style of dress with each new decade.

Make sure you're physically comfortable in your clothes. Don't give up comfort for allure. After all, *you* can look seductive wearing a potato sack. Besides, one of the sexiest things about a Sex Goddess is her ease with her body. Tight shoes mess that up, no matter how pretty they are.

Finally, wear what *you* like. Without even realizing it, you'll create a Sex Goddess look. Fact is, that's true of any woman, as long as her self-esteem is high, her smile is bright, and her confidence in her sexuality is strong. No seductive poses needed!

Games for the Sex Goddess

1) "Presto! Instant Sex Magic!" (see page 117) Nobody plays this game like you!
2) "Princess Pink Day" (see page 126) is a perfect opportunity to share your sex secrets with friends.
3) "Love, Love, and More Love" (see page 134).
4) "The 'I Can't Hear You' Game" (see page 119) may not seem like an activity that will enhance your status as a Sex Goddess, but being worthy of sensual worship means remaining sure of your sexuality. People will do lots to invalidate a woman's sexual process, and this game can help you to rise above such input.

The Out-to-Change-the-World Goddess

This deity, if you only hear her name, seems synonymous with the Activist Goddess. And they *are* a lot alike. But, while they both want to do big things that make a difference, the Feminine Divine represented in this chapter is not political. As you'll see, her approaches and arenas are elsewhere. And though she is, as her name states, out to change the *world*—the whole planet—the realm in which she actually carries out her work is smaller and her endeavors more personal than those of the Activist Goddess. If she wants to help see that people everywhere are cherished and treated with human decency, she will do everything in her power—pray, meditate, read books, become more patient—to become a person who loves and cherishes everyone she meets. If she wants to feed the homeless, she will not try to do so by political lobbying but will hit the streets and feed them herself, or raise funds for a group to do so.

This deity comes in three "flavors." The first is the New Age Goddess. She sees spirits—or at least hopes to—and wants peace, love, and harmony for all. She also longs for the day when people everywhere are blessed by the presence of a resident wise-woman. Ideally, her.

Her tools for achieving these goals range from herbal brews to mud baths to Fairy statues to altars for obscure, ancient deities with powerful-sounding names. (Oh, I can make fun of this Goddess all I want since I'm one myself.) Her list of accoutrements and activities also might include hugs, massage, self-help texts, psychic readings, magical spells, incenses that range from fabulous scents to those that make you gag, and gemstones laid over belly buttons in order to unblock karma. Many a New Age Goddess has reported dialoging with her inner pre-verbal, shame-based, gender-biased diva, who apparently is the source of all her creativity. Reports also include ancient texts on Witchcraft and best-selling texts on people *finding* ancient texts on Witchcraft.

You don't know whether to worship her or to run when you see her coming. Her innovative and sometimes even wacky advice often surprises you because it ends up being exactly what you need to solve your problems. She is optimistic about the worst occurrences, so she can always help you see the bright side. But she *can't* always see that chanting might not be the solution instead of, for example, a government funded health program for all. And sometimes her usual compassion and deep concern for others is replaced by a smug glimmer in her eyes. For instance, when you've got the flu, feel like demons are marching through your sinuses, and you can't take to your bed because your youngest is home from school, ill? That's just when she gets superior and announces, "Now, what did you do to create this situation? Are you making up for past-life karma?"

The second variation on the Out-to-Change-the-World Goddess is the Community Home Goddess, who opens her private dwelling for events that make a difference. Whether it's for a quilting circle for the NAMES Project to commemorate those who have died of AIDS, or a clothing drive for a battered women's shelter, her home is the center of activities that make the world a better place. My friend Ian calls this lifestyle "changing the world from your living room." What's remarkable about this woman— other than her enormous caring and generosity—is that her work has a huge impact. If you actually go into the homes of women like her, you will be stunned to discover that with no budget—and nary a committee to be had—ripples spread out from her hearth that help hundreds if not thousands of people.

Take a lesson from her: don't wait 'til you've got the right building, enough money, inner strength, calm, belief, or sufficient staff. Make a difference *now*. Start small if you want or must. Take on a manageable project so that it is not waylaid by planning that becomes overwhelming in and of itself. But start.

What's divine about the first two variations of the Out-to-Change-the-World-Goddess is that they believe one person can make a difference without being part of a larger organization. They each think, "I alone can change the world." (This characteristic is commendable even in the Goddess of Wrath and Unintentional Destruction, whose chapter comes later in the book.)

I am not against people organizing into large groups. In fact, the third manifestation of the Out-to-Change-the-World-Goddess makes her mark by working in organizations, which is also necessary in this world. But so are people, on their own, with whatever outer and inner resources they have on hand right then and there, trying to do something, large or small. The two aforementioned Out-to-Change-the-World-Goddesses don't think they have to join a group, or fetch coffee for someone else supposedly more capable. Part of why this is praiseworthy is that most people nowadays reading my exhortation to just get started will come up with a reason it's futile to do so.

The final Out-to-Change-the-World-Goddess is Goddess Serious, who is a team player. She likely works in a nonprofit organization, perhaps as a fundraiser or event organizer, but in any number of capacities. Or maybe she doesn't have to work for a living but still heads volunteer committees that work for change. Her deep caring, insistence on making a difference, and tireless devotion are the same as that of her Out-to-Change-the-World sisters. The only difference is her penchant for organizations—she finds them effective, and they suit her temperament.

Lest you confuse Goddess Serious with the Activist Goddess, since the latter also might also work for change within organizations, understand that the former's organization will not be political but focused in a more direct and personal way. For example, Goddess Serious is involved in fundraising not to back a politician, but to finance a health clinic for low income families.

All Out-to-Change-the-World Goddesses know that one must strive for change no matter what. They are good role models for us all. They have such a depth of understanding about world change that they know that even if what we do cannot make a difference, we must try anyway. Gandhi said, "Satisfaction lies in the effort, not in the attainment."

I believe if we do what we can to promote change, eventually critical mass will be reached. But it takes a lot of energy and faith to act in the face of overwhelming evidence that action is futile. The Out-to-Change-the-World-Goddess has perseverance. Even when she doesn't believe in what she's doing, she keeps doing it anyway, until she's regained her belief that it's worthwhile.

Strengths

If you're an Out-to-Change-the-World-Goddess, you've the heart of an angel, filled with concern and good will. Compassion for the suffering of others along with a healthy anger concerning wrongdoing motivate you to try to make a difference in an issue others think might be a lost cause. Your openness to new ways of doing things and your almost unending perseverance will rarely fail you and the people whom you rally.

Weaknesses

You're so busy trying to change things that you don't see when the status quo is working. The way a long-time committee chair does his job, a Yule tradition of your Mom's, a store's return policy—each may have a sound purpose and even depth you don't perceive.

You can be bull-headed, thinking you're the only one who really wants to improve things. That sort of superiority alienates people and keeps them from working with you toward goals you actually have in common.

Cooperation is not your strong point. You need to learn that your ideas may not always be the best way to accomplish something.

You may need to focus more on changing your own life instead of everyone else's.

Ways for the Out-to-Change-the-World-Goddess to Change Her *Own* World

There's not a thing you won't do in order to help someone in need. Unfortunately, it's not always the right thing. A great deal of the time it *is*, but when it's not, it can be a disaster. Don't stop trying to be of service. Just realize that your amazing enthusiasm is a double-edged sword. Know when to temper it a bit and when it's okay to charge forth with it. Yes, it's okay to give that enthusiasm full reign when it's appropriate. And don't let anyone tell you different!

Remarkable visions of how things could be are wonderful. Honor the ideas that come to you; they're special insights that not everyone can offer to their family, friends, and community. But watch out for how you implement these ideas and how you express them to others. The end never justifies the means. More important, unless the means is thoughtfully considerate of others, patient with people's fear of change, and based in an understanding of everyone's remarkably different needs and personalities, the hoped for end result is simply not going to happen.

Finally, be good to yourself in the here-and-now instead of only working on a better tomorrow. Don't lose sight of your day-to-day needs and wishes, or you'll always be one step ahead of yourself. That's no fun.

Fashion Tips

You are busy, so your clothes should be simple, and you want to be well-dressed without too much bother. You need an easy-care and easy to wear wardrobe, and to avoid a fussy look, which doesn't suit your activities.

Find classic styles that'll see you from sewing circle to committee meeting to fundraiser. Bright colors will match your usual optimism and lift your spirits when said optimism flounders.

Pieces with simple lines are easier to mix and match, so that you don't spend hours trying to create an ensemble.

Buy a few elegant, traditional accessories that will go with everything. Think pearls.

If you're a New Age Goddess, the above tips apply to *you*, too. You may enjoy extravagant and mystical styles, so add that sort of accessory. But most of the time keep clothing simple so people take you seriously. Your ideas are so eccentric.

On the other hand, if you don't let loose once in a while you'll go nuts. So don't throw out that silk chiffon ritual robe or stop from buying the full length velvet-lined cape. Just don't wear them every day! Choose when and where, and if that's during a board meeting—well, at least don't dress that way three board meetings in a row.

Games For the Out-to-Change-the-World Goddess

1) "The 'I Can't Hear You' Game" (see page 119) will help preserve your confidence when people attempt to stifle your enthusiasm. And you'll lead the game *so* well!
2) "The Big Secret" (see page 121).
3) Since you tend to be too serious, try "Cosmic Coincidental Fortune Telling Stories" (see page 131). It's also a great way to bond with your fellow Out-to-Change-the-World Goddesses, because it'll help you all let your hair down and get out of work mode. It might even give you guidance about the next step in changing the status-quo or reveal—especially to the New Age Goddesses—the next cosmic act needed on your spiritual path.

The Trickster Goddess

This next Modern Goddess has a knack for causing *necessary* trouble and chaos. This is how it works: she is completely eccentric and unpredictable—her friends and colleagues never know what she'll say, wear, or do. But nine times out of ten, the "wrong" thing she does ends up being exactly what they need, even if it is maddening at the time. For example, she makes the joke that causes people to wince but then to sigh with relief—she's cleared the air for everyone! Or she spills coffee on her friend's new dress right before she leaves on a date. But the friend wasn't really comfortable in that outfit in the first place and ends up looking fabulous in something else.

This prankster might be totally unconscious of her odd ways, the disruption she causes, and their amazing benefits for anyone in her vicinity.

She can be a delight or a horror to those around her, depending on how they decide to deal with her. If people look closely to see the reasons behind her antics and disruptions, they're glad she's around. She's a cosmic force to be reckoned with. All on her own, in her Looney Tunes style, she seems to act for the Gods, madly shifting fate. But if one doesn't learn to grasp the subtle lessons and magnificent benefits her foolishness presents, she may appear to be a curse.

My friend Annie Sprinkle told me about the Goddess of Dissension or the Devil's Advocate Goddess, who causes trouble to people trying to teach a workshop. (I imagine she would have the same impact on, say, managing an office or coordinating a fundraiser.) Annie didn't know who dubbed this Goddess but I suspect she's a type of Trickster Goddess, and as such she must be honored by other Goddesses. This is how I see her: she teaches us to be flexible, to go with the flow and all the lessons in that flow. Her surprises make others learn to take detours, hold steadfast against detours when necessary, and let go of pompousness. She also might teach people to relinquish ideas and patterns that no longer serve a healthy purpose.

Strengths

Sometimes, we can come to a deeply needed truth about ourselves or life only through play, humor, or foolishness. If you're a Trickster Goddess, you help this process along, big time. And, when the conscious mind defends itself, and we primly or with wary ego dare not admit to ourselves our secret needs, feelings, or thoughts, you cause the laughter that surprises us into recognition of these hidden traits, worries, and wonders.

When people are upset, even deeply and legitimately so, laughter can dispel the pain, and even open them up to divine help. Laughter can clear minds, hearts, and spirits of the self-importance and worry that keep us from living freely and happily. You cause this merriment.

You've one of the biggest hearts on the planet. That's what makes your trickery wholesome instead of destructive.

Staying good-humored comes naturally to you. It's not that you don't feel deeply, because you *do*. But you always have the best intentions, and that motivation keeps you cheerful and optimistic.

Weaknesses

If you're not yet an *evolved* Trickster Goddess, or are having a bad day, despite that "biggest heart" I just mentioned, your tomfoolery misses a beat. In other words, you're just plain old annoying. Well, hmm, you're annoying a lot of the time, anyway. You can disrupt things even when it's not helpful, go on verbal tangents when there's *really* no time, and all in all miss the point of what's going on around you.

Your fabulous disregard for convention and propriety sometimes becomes regrettable thoughtlessness. It's not so much the extent to which you go against the norm that makes your pranks work or not. If you're up to snuff, you can pull off anything. But there's a shift that can happen that, slight as it is, makes your tricks turn sour.

You can find it hard to hold down a job because you can't manage to stay in step with all the other 'droids.

Self-Improvement for the Cosmic Trickster

People misunderstand you. So, if you are a sacred fool, thank the Goddess for being such a useful part of society. When one plays the sacred fool, one is the disrupter of order and pretense who helps others not only see themselves better but recognize life's truer values.

Ask yourself if there is some particular way in which you are a sacred trickster. In other words, use a few words to define your own special way of being a fool. Though you've a reputation for a lack of discipline, it's not true. It actually takes a lot of discipline to be a divine fool. But it's atypical discipline (of course!). You go to any lengths to be positive and true to your deepest beliefs. So don't be discouraged by naysayers. When you must achieve a goal that requires you be totally logical, linear, and in step with everyone else, draw on the discipline you already have. It's there. Besides, you *are* quite logical. You just use reason to arrive at different conclusions than most people would.

In the same vein, you're one of the most organized Goddesses around despite your reputation. Your ability to move in, around, and with chaos is only one demonstration of this. For another, it takes a fast, logical thinker to pull off your escapades. So don't listen to anyone who portrays you as just plain old crazy—you're crazy like a fox! Trust your fine intellect, and realize that you integrate it well with a sacred madness. Discipline yourself well enough to recognize when it's best to temporarily forsake the wildness and draw solely on your excellent organizational abilities.

You may want to research Native American lore on Coyote, a traditional sacred trickster. This information could help you gain insights into your place in the scheme of things.

Fashion Tips

Wow, I can sum it up in one sentence: wear whatever you feel like wearing at any given moment. Of course, if I told *you* otherwise, you'd ignore me anyway.

Part of your charm is that you're an amiable split-personality. You aren't actually crazy, but there are a million "you"s inside. And no one will ever be able to guess who the next "you" is going to be!

You dress wildly for weeks on end, and just as everyone gets used to that, you show up in a classic, conservative, Italian business suit, which unsettles them even more than your previous garb, because they're wondering what you're up to *now.*

The only caution I'll add is: when tricks aren't going to get you your way, and you need to make a sober impression, pretend you're a Mother, Corporate, or Girlfriend Goddess, and dress accordingly. Think of it as one big trick. Maybe you'll pass—for about a half hour. Then leave, fast.

Games for the Trickster Goddess

1) "Love, Love, and More Love" (see page 134) is your game if anyone's. It takes a big heart to be the Cosmically Conscious Fool, and it's a harder job than it seems. When you're being true to yourself, your antics are motivated by love, even if it's unconscious. (When you're not true to yourself, your tricks can have a negative effect.) This game combines pure silliness with pure love. What could be a better game for you to play and/or lead? Or a better game to help one become a bit of a trickster if one is not a trickster already?

2) "How to Be (at Least a Bit of) a Bad Girl Goddess, Version #1" (see page 122) is perfect for you, though not because you need to be bad. You can keep up with the most mischievous of the Goddesses. You will like playing or leading this game because it's disruptive!

3) "Cosmic Coincidental Fortune Telling Stories" (see page 131) is also perfect for you, for the same reasons. More, it is a game about embracing chaos as a beneficent guiding force. Perfect!

The Bad Girl Goddess

First, you're not really bad. People just misunderstand you. You *had* to order two servings of the largest, most extravagant dessert on the menu— no one realizes that Goddesses burn more calories than other folks: it takes a lot of energy to run the world.

No Goddess is *really* bad. It's just a matter of style. The so-called rude remark you made was simply meant to enlighten your friend so she could finally get a job she *likes*.

And all that sex you had with your latest beau, even if you had to cancel all other engagements every day for a week? A Goddess has mysterious priorities unknown to lesser beings. And She shouldn't have to explain them!

Strengths

We all need a bit of the bad girl in us, to persuade us to do things occasionally that we might *think* are bad because of foolish things we've been taught. For example, "Good girls don't." Okay, then I'll be bad and enjoy a sex life. Or "Always be nice, nice, nice no matter what." The Bad Girl Goddess might be the only one in the office capable of the fine edged wisecrack that will take the sexist boss down, down, down! We all need to develop at least a bit of the Bad Girl Goddess in us. She lives the life she loves, true to herself every step of the way.

Bad Girl Goddesses can also be incredibly loyal to their loved ones, and will stand and fight to the death for you. And they have the chutzpah and fighting spirit to do it. So if *you're* not a Bad Girl, here's important advice: when you can't quite handle a battle yourself and need a straight-ahead scary bitch on your team—someone to stand up to your bullying boyfriend, irate neighbor, endlessly annoying mother-in-law—figure out who your Bad Girl Goddess friend is, call her on the phone, and she'll come running!

Weaknesses

Aw, c'mon! When you're a Bad Girl Goddess, the flaws are endless. Not that I'm saying one shouldn't care about one's faults, but with this particular deity I couldn't possibly list negative characteristics because they go on forever. But I'll be merciful and name a few pitfalls that one needs to watch for: impulsive acts, headstrong decisions, and, well, never mind. I must be a Bad Girl Goddess because those seem like positive traits.

Just be patient with yourself when your need for impish mischief is irresistible, and try to not let it get out of hand. Remember the following: anything you do as a Bad Girl Goddess, you're responsible for. So make sure that you're willing to pick up the pieces before you make any rash decisions.

Wicked Wisdom for Wild Women

A Bad Girl Goddess may want to tote a gun as a fashion accessory. Don't. It clashes with everything. Besides, it won't attract your dream lover, who, believe it or not, doesn't have a lot of flash and glamour. Not at first. But don't ignore those mild mannered, meek fellows. Many of them turn into a Superman when they take off their horn-rimmed glasses. You just have to give them a chance; and you're exactly the woman to put a fire under them. So just be yourself and let the magic happen.

I know bad boys seem perfect for you, but they'll woo you then leave you high and dry. Despite all your spunk and pizzazz, you don't have what it takes to mate with your male counterpart. He's looking for a sweet girl to tame him. Maybe that's disgusting, but it's his problem, not yours. Unless you foolishly decide to take him on. Heartbreak City.

Fashion Tips

You need to know: you can pull off the absolutely sexiest and/or most outrageous outfits. Regardless of your size, build, or any other physical factor, in your case attitude is all. For example, if you're in a wheel chair, be bad, look bad, smile bad—I've seen it done. I've got one friend who has green hair and a scary attitude. No one gives her trouble, no way, no how. Queen of Bad Girls, she just sits in her throne, rolling along.

Games for the Bad Girl Goddess

If you want to embrace your cosmic aptitude as a Bad Girl Goddess, the following games are for you, as well as games a Bad Girl Goddess might enjoy leading, since it is always oh-so-fulfilling to help others get into a bit of *wholesome* trouble:

1) "Presto! Instant Sex Magic!" (see page 117).
2) "How to Be (at Least a Bit of) a Bad Girl Goddess, Version #1: The Train Wreck Boogie" (see page 122) includes a tune with lyrics that Thelma and Louise would have loved.
3) "How to Be (at Least a Bit of) a Bad Girl Goddess, Version #2" (see page 124).

The Princess Goddess

This deity understands that *princess* is a verb. I princess, you princess, and she *really* princesses.

When I was a little girl I wanted to be a princess. I finally confessed that to my therapist who, believe it or not, informed me it was a perfectly reasonable goal. Since then, I've been on the road to princessdom—carried on a litter, of course, by gorgeous, enamored men.

It was hard at first because I don't come from money, and just you *try* to get a scholarship for princess training school. Therefore, so that you needn't suffer as I did, I provide three princess games without the high cost that most princess schools would exact! But before we get to the games, we had better understand the full benefits of playing them by getting to know this deity better. So:

Strengths

Included in the better parts of this royal deity are grace, graciousness, impeccable taste, lavish generosity with material goods, and strong self-respect. In a crisis, she's resourceful, considerate, and reliable, whether it's the crisis of a personal friend or that of a nation. She's also articulate, usually has an excellent understanding of fine arts, and may have an artistic streak herself. Her interest is piqued by any number of topics and kinds of people. She is the perfect hostess. She has the ability to produce the most lavish yet utterly tasteful event. She also has the knack for making the simplest event feel extravagant, even if the menu is one part peanut butter, one part jelly, and two parts bread.

Weaknesses

On the other hand, the Princess Goddess can be petulant, self-indulgent, oblivious to others' hardships, and hard of hearing when it comes to criticism. She can demonstrate a terrible temper and hold a grudge better than Lucy when Ricky would tell her "No, you *can't* be in my show!" Her innate artistry often either remains undeveloped or, if expressed, is done privately so others don't see it. It is by no means a fault to keep art as a private hobby. Art is like sex: some people like it private and those of us who are, artistically speaking, whores, show all, to all. But the problem with the Princess Goddess is that she resents those who commit to their art enough to publicly display it, and who therefore, also, suffer the sacrifices necessary to do so. The Princess Goddess in her jealousy might hurt the more vulnerable artists in her vicinity.

Finally, she might forget that life is not a show. It's to be lived, not performed. So, she might forget that, especially for her, the best art is living high—lushly and kindly.

Helpful Hints for Her Highness

It's difficult to give a princess advice. You're not likely to listen. So my first helpful hint is: listen! If you are doing so now, I will proceed:

Whenever you're feeling like a princess, it is an excellent time for self-indulgence and/or charity work. That might seem like a contradiction to some but not to *your* regal mindset.

You've got the cosmic attitude needed to be wonderfully guilt free should you spend an hour in a bubble bath, follow it with lunch at a high-end restaurant, after which you go home for a long nap, and then enjoy a marathon movie binge consisting of three or four romantic comedies without any redeeming value.

However, you might find instead that largess comes to you naturally. If so, take advantage of it. The world needs all the help it can get, and you'll discover yourself particularly effective when you try to make a difference.

Of course, a princess easily alternates between the two extremes: pampering herself and giving to others. Perhaps you can take that long bath, then discuss a new charity project over that sumptuous lunch, then forsake your nap to help a friend in need, after which you proceed to your movie marathon.

If there's a Goddess who's schizophrenic, it's you. Generous/selfish, compassionate/stuck-up, loyal/fickle, and so on. No one's more loyal or more fickle. More generous or more selfish. How do you do it? I don't know. But I know this: you should love yourself and honor all your strange, strange convolutions. They do make sense, in their own way, and add up to a grandeur of heart and personality that is loveable and an important force in the lives of everyone around you.

I know you are really afraid to do otherwise, but get rid of your A list/B list way of doing things. You know better and want to change, so it's only a matter of getting over your fear. Of course, *only a matter of getting over your fear* might seem an inappropriate choice of words, as huge as your fear may be, but it's all that is standing in your way. And it's not an insurmountable obstacle. Furthermore, once you're over that hurdle, you'll be rewarded with love from so many more people.

Finally, don't try to go it alone so much; being a princess in her high lonely tower keeps you from inner and outer change. Be brave, and dare to come down, Rapunzel. It's springtime and the flowers are in bloom. You must see them. I'll get a ladder.

Fashion Tips

Consider being more bold in your fashion statements. Royalty can be so conservative in their dress, yet you have the grace, elegance and ease to carry off just about any outfit. On the other hand, if you *do* choose to dress like the '60s never happened, you're the person who can pull it off. So do it to the hilt!

Games for the Princess Goddess

1) "Princess Pink Day" (see page 126) provides the indulgence that royalty, and those hoping to be royalty, require.

2) "The Big Secret" (see page 121) adds grace to Her Graciousness. And if you don't already own that title, this game will help you do so. As will the next one.

3) "Love, Love, and More Love" (see page 134) fosters the, well, love, love, and more love that is part and parcel of regal living.

The Goddess of Wrath and Unintentional Destruction

The Goddess of Wrath and Unintentional Destruction really wants to make things better but somehow just can't help but upset the apple cart.

It's easy to see how she got her nickname, *Goddess Unintentional*: for one thing, her indignation tends to seem misplaced. I mean, this is the sort of woman who writes letter after letter to the editor because there's never enough glitter in glitter nail polish! Try as she will, she'd be better off renouncing world change and getting a job on a demolition crew.

On the other hand, her fiery personality occasionally ignites when everyone else is frozen in indifference. She leaps into battle and, even if her efforts prove to be ineffective, at least draws attention to the problem at hand.

And, bless her big heart, she always sees the position of the underdog, with quickly dispensed compassion, solace, and support.

She often has had a lot of unkindness dealt her. This is part of what makes her anger quick to flare. Yet, the unkindness she has experienced has not snuffed out her spirit. Her rants and raves and rages prove that. As such, she represents the unquenchable female power.

It's important to point out that the Goddess of Wrath and Unintentional Destruction, unlike the other divinities in this book, does not represent a woman as a whole. In other words, she is a *part* of some women, smaller or larger, as the case may be. She may come into existence only a few times in some women's life, if at all. Though I've said that most women are many Goddesses rolled into one female, it's more the case here. To think otherwise implies that that's all there is in a woman who's a Goddess of Wrath and Unintentional Destruction.

But, almost always, she has a lot of other, equally strong facets. She may be a fine Mother Goddess, patiently, carefully, and effectively home-schooling her children. Or perhaps she's a Love Goddess who only goes on a tirade once a year, when her heart can no longer be patient with life's cruelties.

She could even be an aspect of a woman who is an Activist Goddess. I've talked about both possibly losing their tempers. But with Goddess Unintentional it's an ongoing event; if she's on the horizon, so is a rant; it defines her to a great extent, and constantly causes her to make a mess of things. Whereas the Activist Goddess is highly effective and may be a woman whose anger is only part of the picture—a part that is sometimes useful, sometimes detrimental. Even when it's gotten the better of her, it still might not cause the chaos and problems Goddess Unintentional leaves in her wake. Activist Goddess might merely lose her tact or get grumpy.

However, when her temper gets so out of hand that she's really botching the job, then she's experiencing a woman's ability to shift from being one Goddess to another. *Voilà*, Goddess of Wrath and Unintentional Destruction. Who is important to acknowledge as a Goddess in and of herself so that when she appears—within us or in others—we know how to deal with her.

So, though my description of her is not as flattering as that of other Goddesses, it's because she's more an *aspect* of women than she is the *whole* woman.

I also need to make it clear that this deity is an aspect of Kali, the Indian Goddess whose anger and destructiveness are sacred. Life has cycles in which creation and destruction are balanced, building and destroying alternately, creating a dynamic necessary not only for mundane and spiritual growth, but for survival. The Goddess of Wrath and Unintentional Destruction is truly and thoroughly a Goddess and deserves our respect as such.

But Kali's temper is not always so poorly used as the anger of this section's Goddess—she just can't get the hang of it. I guess in a way she does accomplish Kali's job, which is to destroy, but ideally it would be nice if this were done when it was really needed, and not so, well, *destructively*.

Okay, we could argue that all destruction is Kali's and therefore sacred, and that it all has its spiritual lessons and its value in the cycle of life.

And I'd be the first to support that point of view.

But, as much as all that needs to be noted, and as much as it helps us give full respect to Goddess of Wrath and Unintentional Destruction in ourselves and others, right now it could also distract us from the fact that we need to notice if we lose our better judgment, so that our tempers and attempts to improve circumstances don't backfire on us.

So if you find yourself too often Ms. Goddess Unintentional, here are some remedies.

* Practice yoga or another form of meditation so that you learn to go with the flow instead of flying off the handle.
* Do what's needed to find and heal the hidden hurts that fuel your rage.
* Research Kali. Learning about her might help you channel anger more constructively.
* Honor your anger as your cry of "I'm still here, kicking!"
* Know you're a Goddess! You are an important, sincere, caring Goddess. I am sure of it.

The Ultimate Goddess

This deity is the last of the thirteen modern Goddesses discussed. And here is where we get to explore at even greater depth the unique woman *you* are—the Ultimate Goddess.

Every minute of every day, we are a different Goddess and become as many different deities as there are moments in time. But to better enjoy and fully wield that power, we have to recognize it.

It is simple to do so. If you're cooking a meal, realize you're a Cooking Goddess. When you are on the freeway to the office, call yourself a

Commuting Goddess. Whatever you're up to, you're doing it divinely!

Now, don't just read all the above, say, "Wow, that makes me feel good," and stop there.

Keep feeling good by applying what you've read. Goddesses learn that practice, not theory, is what makes a difference. Over the next few days, when you think of it, and then whenever after you want, dub yourself "Goddess" and somehow add your immediate activity to your godly title.

If you become stymied trying to create your appellations, here are some suggestions:

* Add a word or phrase before *Goddess*. It can be an activity or description: Typing Goddess. Vacationing Goddess. Overworked Goddess. Delighted Goddess. Getting-Dressed-to-Take-on-the-World Goddess.
* Try a word or phrase after *Goddess Who*: Goddess Who Teaches. Goddess Who Is On a Deadline. Goddess Who is Running about on Errands So That Her Party is Great!
* Use *Goddess of*: Goddess of the Marketing Department. Goddess of Creativity. Goddess of Shopping. Goddess of Sculpting.
* Add Goddess to your job title: Office Assistant Goddess. Bus Driver Goddess. Real Estate Agent Goddess.
* Or do whatever else strikes your fancy. But try this exercise for a few days, regardless. You may be surprised by how good it can make you feel.

If you want, you can explore the Ultimate Goddess even further. As stated earlier, every woman has dominant traits that reveal that woman's main Goddess type. So the Ultimate Goddess can be defined not only by your shifts and changes throughout your day (and life), but also by who you tend to be consistently, as a whole. And you know best who that is. So, make up yet more of your own Goddesses! If your life is mostly about gardening, perhaps you're the Green Thumb Earth Goddess (or whatever you choose to call yourself.) If you are prone to insightful analysis about literature, have read so many texts about psychology that there's no room on your book shelves any more for your mate's detective novels, and write long epic poems about dieting, hair salons, grocery lists, and self-confidence, dub yourself appropriately. Perhaps "She Who Sees and Knows All"? If you've spent the better part of the last five years making seasonal decorations, children's costumes, beaded belts, and costume jewelry, you might honor your far-ranging arts 'n' crafts abilities by calling yourself "Goddess of the Glue Gun" or whatever title seems to summarize your activities.

Once again, since women are all so multifaceted, you might find that there are several types of Goddess that you tend to embody.

Making up one or several of your own does not invalidate your identification with Goddesses I've defined in previous chapters.

The following are some thoughts for when it's particularly hard to recognize your divinity.

Even if what you are doing, feeling, or being seems the farthest thing in the world from what you think of as divine, somehow just name yourself "Goddess" at those times. Even if it doesn't seem like it, no matter what you are feeling or doing, you are a Goddess. Honor yourself as one.

After all, any overworked woman who has stood in her home, eyes tearing as she desperately wishes aliens would kidnap her entire family—and then still resolutely walks into the bedroom because an ailing child, parent, or spouse needs a glass of water—deserves all our worship!

Of course, it can be hard to see oneself as a good person, let alone divine, when one is depressed or angry. But all the more reason to honor yourself then, even if, logically speaking, you could make a good argument that you're the essence of "bad." Kali, the Indian Goddess, is known for Her wrath. So are deities throughout the world. And don't tell me, "Yeah, but that's all *good* anger." Nobody's perfect, not even we Goddesses.

Illness or PMS can also make you doubt your divinity. Don't. One thing ancient Goddess worshippers understood is that life has cycles. Life, death, rebirth. Health, illness, recovery. They saw the Goddess as a reflection of these cycles. Women also reflect the very same patterns.

Christian mystics speak of "consolation" and "desolation." Consolation is when you feel connected to God, your meditations are a joy to do, and you're on top of the world. Desolation is when you feel miserable and trapped in a Godless world, and you can't even make the effort to feel better. What's stunning is that they also believe that both consolation and desolation are inevitable in a spiritual journey. And whether you're into spirituality or not, you can still use the wisdom of these Christian mystics: If being a complete pill (for want of a better term) is an unavoidable part of spiritual life, then none of us need feel unspiritual, or bad, or less than divine when we're down, lost, desolate, or temporarily giving up. At such times, we're simply Lost Goddesses. Or Desolate Goddesses. Or Mopey Goddesses. Or...

Thank goodness for our deep flaws because, if we are honest enough to acknowledge them, they keep us humble. They help us see that, well, even Goddesses are only human. We're so powerful on the one hand and on the other so fragile and so terribly capable of mistakes.

Humility isn't the same as beating ourselves up and feeling bad about ourselves. Humility allows us to admit our failings because it tells us "You're only human. It is inevitable you'll make mistakes. Don't hate yourself for it. God(dess) doesn't!" Humility also informs us that, since we're not perfect, we need the help of other people instead of trying to go it all alone.

Love yourself for who you are, and do it all the more when you are not living up to your own expectations. Love, not browbeating, heals us so that we can be better people. I am not implying that one needn't do their absolute best to be a good person. We Goddesses have to be very disciplined in the pursuit of improving ourselves, so that we will use our divine powers for good, and be kind, giving, and effective people. But I will absolutely insist that no matter how hard a person tries, she'll be far from perfect. Very far. And if she deludes herself either by thinking she's fault-free or that she *should* be, misery's ahead for her and everyone around her.

Sometimes, we might fail in ways that deeply shame us. Even then, love, not self-hatred, helps us to make the needed reparations—whether to self or others—and to improve. Love also helps us move on, staying engaged in life. Don't retreat when you fall down! You are really needed in this nuthouse called life!

If you get stuck and just can't feel good about yourself, here's a technique I teach in my Goddess Spirituality classes. Think of one thing inside yourself that keeps you from seeing yourself as a Goddess. Here are examples of such inner blocks. The belief "I am not big enough to make a difference in the world." Or "I am not beautiful enough to be a Goddess." Or the fear that people will laugh at you if you think *you* could be as powerful as a Goddess.

Then, using your imagination, send your inner block down to Mother Earth. Send it DOWN into the earth, so it doesn't bother you anymore. When we are free of our self-doubt and fears, the GREAT GODDESS who runs the show emerges from within us, and we can create the world of our dreams! If you find yourself laughing as you use this technique, that's okay. Why not?

Here's another helpful tool when you're abysmally doubting your worth, let alone your divinity. Women often put on their makeup while giving themselves the most negative messages: "I have to put on this lip-stick so I'll be pretty." "If I don't use eyeliner my eyes look like a pig's." "I need makeup or no one will ask me out on a date."

Argh! The next time you're in front of the mirror with a lipstick, eye-liner, or mascara brush in hand, try reversing this. As you apply the makeup, tell yourself, "I am adorning the beautiful Goddess that I am, beautiful inside and out."

It might feel silly. But it's an effective way to come into an appreciation of your worth, dignity, and loveliness.

Moving onto another topic: when planning this book, I decided not to include a chapter on Goddesses who embody, above and beyond anything else, the eccentric personality. I also left out a section on Goddesses who are artists, singers, dancers, or the like.

After all, if a woman is eccentric, she isn't going to totally fit any of this book's Goddess descriptions. That's the definition of eccentricity. Yes, I realize that no woman is truly defined by any of my specifications and quizzes. We're all too unique and multifaceted for that. But the eccentric is going to more stubbornly, I mean assertively, insist that no quiz could ever define *her*.

As for the artistic personality, she is often eccentric so will be just as stubborn, um, I really do mean *assertive* about this matter. Except, perhaps, even more so, because, being creative, she'll want to write her own quiz, thank you very much.

So this chapter is a chance for artists and eccentrics to go hog-wild cre-atively, with divine self-definitions. In any case, everyone, in my opinion, is, if not eccentric, unique unto themselves. This section is a chance for each woman to further celebrate herself as divinely inspired. Just follow this section's instructions for discovering the unique Goddess you are. Because that's the Ultimate Goddess.

The Goddess in the Mirror

A woman's divinity can be hidden, suppressed, frightened, cowed. But it's there; nothing will change that about a woman. It's there, ready and waiting to express its power and beauty. Godliness is eternal and will eventually manifest itself, although maybe in surprising ways that do not at first seem godlike, but that time will prove valuable and magnificent.

When that innate dignity, vigor, and strength is hushed up and pushed down, it still functions deep within. It works its gift within you until it blooms.

It might bloom in rage, if it's been ignored long enough. If battered, it might come forth haltingly, shyly, or awkwardly. Then it is a Raging Goddess, Halting Goddess, Shy or Awkward Goddess. Name it to claim its power.

Again, you are a Goddess, and there is *nothing* that changes that about a woman. I am physically disabled. So the Goddess I am gets to find her strength through the challenges of physical pain and limited activity. Hey, just as I wrote that, I figured out why my doctor said today that I am strong. And it's totally to the point of what I'm trying to say.

He said I'm strong. When I objected, he countered with "You're not strong physically but emotionally, spiritually."

As I explained to him, I do not consider myself strong spiritually. My biggest strength in that regard, in fact, is that I know I'm weak and have to rely on the Goddess, because otherwise I don't have what it takes to either accomplish what I want or find serenity in this crazy world.

But now I know what he meant—despite my disability, because I know I need to rely on my Goddess, I stay connected to my inner Goddess, as well as to the Goddess who is my creator. These spiritual connections keep me from seeing myself solely as disabled—I keep going, keep writing, teach class from bed when I have to, have friends type my manuscripts, and keep my life going. I don't give up. And one could call that spiritual strength.

I'm so excited. I get what he was saying now. I must be a Goddess! I feel great.

Please always know you're one, too. Some days, when I'm doing my physical therapy, it gets lonely knowing a lot of other women aren't acknowledging their power. My doctor says 70 percent of the people with my current physical problem get into bed and end their lives, doing nothing for the rest of their days. It's been a year and a half since my own disability hit; I am still working and bit by bit healing the disability. But the therapy workout is really hard to keep doing every day because it's quite lengthy and sometimes painful. I don't like to feel alone in it. So please, I'm not just saying the following to make a point, know you're a Goddess for my sake.

And I sincerely promise to keep knowing it about myself so that you don't feel lonely facing your own challenges.

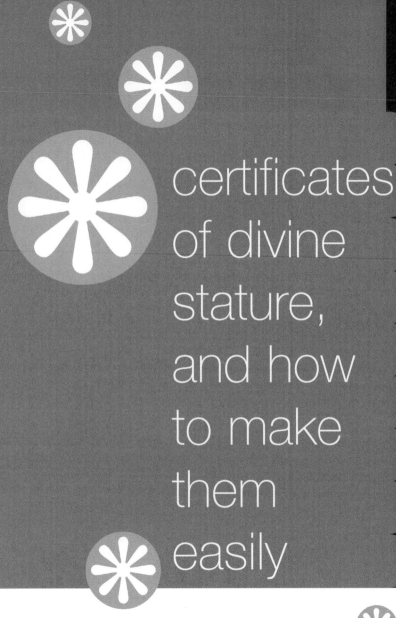

certificates
of divine
stature,
and how
to make
them
 easily

ertificates for each Goddess are easy to make. These can be bestowed upon friends, as party favors, or to boost someone when they are feeling low or lacking self-confidence. Or they can be given just for fun. A friend needn't have read or even known about this book to enjoy having her divine presence acknowledged through official certification. And don't forget to give yourself one. After all, if you don't worship yourself, no one else will!

Simply type or hand letter, "This document certifies that (*fill in name*) is a bona fide (*fill in type of*) Goddess, worthy of all the cosmic powers, privileges, and homage due to one of her divine stature." If you don't know which type of Goddess it would be best to call your friend, don't make that part of the certificate. Have it simply read "...a bona fide Goddess," which is pretty classy all by itself.

Of course, you may want to go the whole nine yards, buying certificate paper from a stationery store and using a fabulous computer font. But whatever font, handwriting, or paper you usually use is fine, and the simple version is sure to give you or your friend a boost (and a giggle!).

Framing is optional. A nice presentation is to roll up the certificate and tie a pretty ribbon around it.

Do read the chapter, "How To Have a Goddess Party." It will give you an excuse to make the certificates, as well as other ideas for celebrating your superhuman qualities.

goddess
compatibility
(and how
we can all
live in divine
harmony)

We Goddesses have more power if we cooperate and combine our cosmic efforts. We should leave the infighting to the God-Guys. Kidding aside, men can be awfully good team players. So let's emulate them. This chapter shows how to best get along with other Goddesses.

Goddesses have a lot to learn from each other. And we can all join one another in a grand female conspiracy if we know what the pitfalls might be. Let's look at both the compatibilities *and* the incompatibilities of all the Goddesses; this will help us navigate any possibly rocky grounds.

I've given each Goddess her own section in this chapter. Also, a deity is often discussed outside her own section, in which case I've bolded her name. Using the bolded print you can find anyone with a quick perusal. Some of the Goddesses have shorter sections. Don't be put off by that. Each deity is amply covered, if not in her own section then in others. Just search for the bolded names. If you are interested in how you stand with a particular Goddess, and in glancing at her section you don't see your Goddess type bolded, read the section anyway. There might be relevant info about you, just not by name.

Mother Goddess Compatibility

The Mother Goddess can be in harmony with almost all other Goddesses as long as she feels useful to them and appreciated. So if you are, for example, **Goddess-Just-Wants-to-Have-Fun**, remember to thank your mother for doing your laundry while you were busy out at the clubs!

Princess Goddess, if you want pampering, go to the Mother Goddess. Just be ready to take a scolding whenever she sees you lacking noblesse oblige.

Trickster Goddess can be particularly trying for the Mother when the latter needs to be a force of love in its most organized and perhaps plodding expression. When they both realize that they are expressing the same love, but in different ways, cooperation is more likely. If that realization doesn't work, a pie fight might. But only after Trickster has helped Mother with her work, and done so in a timely manner. *And* if Trickster cleans up the pie.

Goddess of Love and Mother Goddess occasionally bump heads. They're both so kind-hearted and serving that they get in each other's way. If they acknowledge the reason for this conflict, they'll be less annoyed with each other. Then when the subject comes up again, they can immediately divvy up the territory as to who is going to do what.

Of course, if they start getting competitive about which of the two is more loving, giving, and gracious, well, girlfriend, it's ugly. Do you hear me? They become petty, backbiting, and so scary that everyone else leaves the premises.

Solution: They, too, should leave the premises, until they cool off. Then they should either:

a) Get drunk (but, heaven help us, not together);

b) Enjoy a book or movie, but *not* something about a self-sacrificing, noble caregiver or other character whose story will drown Mother or Love Goddess in self-pity and indignation; or

c) First get drunk (or at least go work out at the gym, or run around the block, or do thirty jumping jacks—anything to blow off steam so as to be better able to listen), then go talk with a counselor, priest, witch, rabbi, minister, shaman, psychic, priestess, mother, sister, best friend, or anyone else who'll tell it to them square: "Love is not a competitive sport. You love for the sake of loving. If your self-worth comes from loving others, you need to change." Then they should go to whichever counselor, priest, witch, rabbi, minister, shaman, psychic, priestess, mother, sister, best friend who can show them how to implement those changes.

By the way, the **Corporate Goddess** can be a great counselor in this situation if she's learned the way business people cooperate to achieve their career goals. Cooperation is something men as a group really have down—at least among themselves—so it permeates the business industry. If the Corporate Goddess has learned this skill, she's a real resource for other women.

Corporate Goddess Compatibility

The Corporate Goddess might not get along with any of the other Goddesses, if she sees them as too dependent on men or financially naive. She needs to remember that any woman, in any life style, is strong. It's our nature! The deity of business and the **Goddess of Love** have a lot to teach each other. If they can get past any initial antipathy—and it'll be there—their very different views and approaches actually complement each other. The Love Goddess mellows out the Business Queen and teaches her new priorities. The Corporate Goddess gives back with down-to-earth lessons in money matters and can reveal why love needn't always mean sacrifice.

Goddess-Just-Wants-to-Have-Fun can help Corporate Goddess a lot. Our Cosmic Businesswoman might need not-so-serious instruction about how *not* to buckle down. If these two hang out and share some girlfriend time, Corporate Goddess might learn how to let loose, grin bigger, and relax. In the same vein, she can teach Goddess-Just-Wants-to-Have-Fun some seriousness.

Bad Girl Goddess Compatibility

It may surprise you to find out who loves Bad Girl Goddess and who doesn't. **Mother Goddess** and she often hit it off. The maternal urge to scold can be thoroughly fulfilled when Bad Girl gets up to no good, and Bad Girl, in return, adores the unconditional nurturing and acceptance Mother Goddess doles out so generously. **Activist Goddess** finds she can often enlist Bad Girl for the more radical and risky escapades social change requires. And **Sex Goddess**, well, no surprise that there's compatibility there.

You would think **Trickster** and Bad Girl Goddesses would be great friends. But our cosmically foolish divinity of chaos has a serious streak to her—there's a method to her mischief. Thus, in comparison to herself, she finds Bad Girl low-content. The Trickster Goddess needs to realize that, sometimes, tomfoolery can happen just for its own sake. It is plain old fun and doesn't need to have her trickster agenda. But she's loved by the Bad Girl Goddess anyway, who enjoys anyone disruptively creative.

Bad Girl Goddess can get along great guns with the **Out-to-Change-the-World-Goddess**. The two of them can indulge in all sorts of trouble together, because they'll both feel fine about it. They both see the value of shaking things up.

The other gals sometimes find the Bad Girl Goddess a bit frightening because she symbolizes a part of themselves that they long to express but often keep well hidden. The **Princess Goddess**, however—get her drunk and she's Bad Girl Goddess all the way!

Activist Goddess Compatibility

Activist Goddess can have a hard time with the **Corporate Goddess, Mother Goddess, Sex Goddess,** or **Goddess-Just-Wants-to-Have-Fun.** She might think them shallow or selfish. To achieve harmony, all she has to do is remember that they all need her. She is creating a world in which they can be strong and free. She also needs *them.* These other women hold down the fort while she's gallivanting about on her crusades. The Mother Goddess, for example, keeps the activist fed and loved, while the Corporate Goddess sees there's food, clothing, etc., around when all is said and done.

It can be hard for *anyone* to get along with the Activist Goddess if you don't understand what drives her. The Activist Goddess seems to find fault with everything, and no one seems to measure up to her standards. Remembering that she is a driven woman can help. Think of how driven a woman can be to mate or to fend for her children. Activist Goddess mates with her causes, and all people are her children. She's trying to do good for you. She just might lack finesse or social skills at times.

The **Out-to-Change-the-World-Goddess** and Activist Goddess have so much in common. You would think they'd be best friends. And they often are. But they also both tend to be set in their ways. Sometimes their resoluteness becomes stubbornness, and when it does they're better off with more mellow, flexible companions with whom they won't have to lock horns. **Trickster Goddess** often has that easy-going quality, because she is so loving and accepting of chaos.

I mentioned earlier an RSVP I received from one of my favorite Activist Goddesses who couldn't come to my party because of political commitments, including possible imprisonment as a result of her upcoming rally. It's a bit startling to receive a note like that if recurring face-offs with police are not something written in your own calendar. Support your Activist Goddess, anyway. Show understanding and love. She needs it, for hers is a challenging path, making her need all the help she can get. Whether you believe in her tactics, or even her goals, we're all in this together, each contributing our own special piece to the puzzle, even if at times it seems that such disparate pieces will never fit together. Just be kind, courteous, loving.

In the case of the aforementioned RSVP, I wrote back, "You are in my prayers....I will be in the upcoming S.F. voter march, to which I will bring homemade chocolate truffles from the party, in hopes I can feed them to you."

Sex Goddess Compatibility

The Sex Goddess is very popular with other Goddesses, as long as she shares her makeup secrets and doesn't cancel coffee with her gal friends at the last minute just because a cute prospect shows up!

Most female deities might disapprove of the Professional Sex Goddess, because they think that sex should be about love, not about love of one's job. But **Mother Goddess** is different. She, in her infinite, down-to-earth warmth, would simply give a stripper a maternal pat on the head and say, "My, what a good dance routine you did today. Are you tired? Would you like a nice cup of tea?"

And **Activist Goddess** might respond to *any* type of Sex Goddess either by ranting in moral indignation or by seeing these sensual deities as emblems of freedom and social change.

Turn to the Advice Goddess aspect of Mother Goddess if you find yourself jealous of a Sex Goddess, or need advice about getting along with *any* type of Goddess. I always ask my inner Advice Goddess what to do, which often makes me feel like I'm channeling Ms. Manners. When in doubt, remember: the Advice Goddess can give advice on *anything!* And she understands how important it is that we employ courtesy and the willingness to trust that every type of Goddess is playing an important role in the scheme of things. Trust your Advice Goddess, and the Professional Sex Goddess will soon be giving you tips on how to do stripteases for your lover.

Goddess of Love Compatibility

The Goddess of Love of course loves *everyone*. But the other Goddesses don't always love her! Her kindness and generosity make her so popular that other gals might get jealous. Then they have to find the Goddess of Love within themselves so that they are not petty or unkind.

The Goddess of Love and the **Activist Goddess** do particularly well with each other: they both want to help all people everywhere.

Bad Girl Goddess finds Goddess of Love incredibly annoying, because deep inside every Bad Girl is a Goddess of Love waiting to emerge. So, Ms. B.G.G., don't fight it. Take lessons from the women who love, and perhaps help them, in turn, get bad!

Trickster Goddess is particularly dear to Goddess *d'Amour*. The former is endlessly amusing to the latter, who sees the Trickster's nonsense for what it is—pure love embodied in pure laughter.

Goddess of Love also cherishes **Girlfriend Goddess**, with her need to serve, and her often heartsick feeling that no one will serve her in return. Goddess of Love comes to the rescue, with a sincere desire to fill that emptiness right up!

Girlfriend Goddess Compatibility

The Girlfriend Goddess gets along with all Goddesses because she is always there when they need her. But compatibility dwindles if she lives only for them and has no life of her own. Then she gets jealous and grumpy. Antidote: don't always be the helper. Sometimes be a **Sex Goddess**! And hang out with **Bad Girl Goddess** more often. You're too good.

Princess Goddess Compatibility

The Princess Goddess can be difficult for anyone who does not know how to respond to "You *do* understand that my simply *being* here is a luxury item for you? *Don't* you?"

She bumps heads terribly with the **Out-to-Change-the-World-Goddess**, who finds material indulgences offensive, even though she dearly wants them herself and envies the Princess Goddess. The latter, in turn, can easily become guilt-ridden when Out-to-Change-the-World-Goddess comes gallivanting along, exposing life's inequities. The solution: eating together, consuming the richest ice cream topped with the thickest, most decadent chocolate syrup possible and sprinkled with nuts. A bit later, after their blood sugar drops and they both begin to feel guilty at this completely hedonistic extravagance, they will also start sharing their truths honestly with each other. As women do only with chocolate and low blood sugar. Having thus bonded, these two can go out and save the world, arm in arm.

Girlfriend Goddess has to watch that the Princess Goddess doesn't take advantage of her. Being prone to terribly obscure maladies that somehow always make her unable to fend for herself, Princess Goddess can easily rope the all-giving, loyal Girlfriend into becoming the perpetual maid. Remember, Girlfriend Goddess, maid should be a *paid* position. Don't fall for the Princess Goddess's constant so-called needs. In fact, mimic her. Tell her that your Aunt Fifi just left you her fortune, and the news has upset you terribly because it means your poverty-stricken sister must now continue unaided, which makes you feel faint because you are so sensitive. Then climb into that four-poster canopied bed with bed-ridden Princess Goddess, and share her organic chocolates, while watching DVDs on her wall-size television screen.

Out-to-Change-the-World-Goddess Compatibility

The Out-to-Change-the-World-Goddess gets along with all the other deities. Sometimes. The rest of the time she doesn't. Both loveable and impossible, this dynamic, impulsive Diva-of-Change-and-World-Betterment is best approached thoughtfully. In order not to be driven crazy by her faults, dwell as much as you can on her good traits. She has a lot of them. Also, learn to smile vapidly while nodding your head up and down during her rants. It'll keep her from going on longer and longer, and give you something to do instead of scream. **Goddess of Love**, give this gal all you can. She is under-appreciated. When it comes to the care, feeding, and hugging of the Out-to-Change-the-World-Goddess, **Girl-friend Goddess** is excellent. The former's obvious struggles mirror the latter's quieter problems, so they tend to understand each other, though outwardly they're quite different.

Goddess-Just-Wants-to-Have-Fun Compatibility

Goddess-Just-Wants-to-Have-Fun (call her *Goddess Fun* for short) is great pals with the **Girlfriend Goddess**. The latter enjoys going along for the ride when the former goes out to play. And while the Girlfriend Goddess scurries about helping Goddess Fun get ready for pleasure and excitement, Goddess Fun provides payback with tips on makeup, dating, and the latest clubs.

Goddess Fun also can be good pals with **Princess Goddess**, **Sex Goddess**, and, of course, **Bad Girl Goddess**. When they get together, I want to be there, too.

Out-to-Change-the-World-Goddess, if she's the New Age version, gets along fine with Goddess Fun, who for some reason has a penchant for meditation classes, yoga, and sweat lodges.

The other Goddesses can have an awfully hard time with Goddess-Just-Wants-To-Have-Fun. None of them finds her serious enough, and they wish she could be at least a bit more responsible. If Goddess Fun is making you batty, phone your Advice Goddess—or channel your own inner Advice Goddess—for a solution. Courtesy, if it is based on kindness and consideration, can often bring harmony to an otherwise impossibly trying situation. Your Advice Goddess will show you how to apply courtesy properly.

Trickster Goddess Compatibility

Trickster Goddess is needed by all the other deities, so that none of them get too stuck in their own routines. Her antics shake them out of complacencies, pompousness, blind spots, and bad moods.

But the various Goddesses have different degrees of appreciation for what she brings to the mix. Often, the more serious deities—**Corporate**, **Activist**, and **Out-to-Change-the-World Goddesses**—feel their sister Trickster is undermining their important efforts. And if she goes too far, she actually *does*. But usually she's, in fact, helping. Other Goddesses have a better relationship with her if they foster appreciation and dwell on the fact that, by introducing the elements of surprise, laughter, or foolishness, Trickster Goddess makes their overly rigid plans more flexible and relevant to people's real and immediate needs.

The **Princess** and Trickster Goddesses have a unique relationship. Historically, royalty has always had a fool in the court. Today, that tradition still holds, the Trickster Goddess being the only person who mocks regal action with complete impunity. No matter how off-the-wall the antics become, and how crazy they make her, the Princess Goddess will suffer them, usually with silent dignity. She knows, deep down, that *someone* has to hold her regal ego in check and her enormous charisma accountable. The Trickster Goddess needs immunity in order to do that job.

Courtesy, Compassion, Acceptance, and... Vampire Slayers?

Since I mentioned three times that courtesy is crucial to harmony between deities, you can call me Goddess Nag—as long as you do so reverently.

If you know the ancient Greek myths about all the troubles on Mt. Olympus, residence of Gods and Goddesses, you realize that someone didn't raise those divinities well at all. Squabbling, petty revenge, and grudges abounded. But you, my reader, are the updated Divinity, with this handy-dandy modern Goddess-guide helping you. I'll finish my treatise on courtesy with this: any two Goddesses can get along if they combine courtesy, compassion, and acceptance.

It is vital that we all learn to support each other.

In the final episode of *Buffy the Vampire Slayer*—a show about a Goddess if there ever was one—Buffy convinces her witch friend, Willow, to try to magically bring all potential vampire slayers into their full power. As such, they'll all have Buffy's superhuman strength and her ability to withstand physical trauma. With so many super-heroes, evil will finally be defeated.

Buffy has, through season after season, felt lonely and isolated. As the only slayer, it is up to her alone to make the decisions and take the actions needed to prevent the spawns of hell from overtaking the earth and destroying humankind. The weight of her responsibilities repeatedly demands she stand apart, unable to share her burden.

At the show's end, having helped empower women all over the world to become vampire slayers, Buffy is no longer alone. Even Willow, in the process of performing her spell, comes into her own super-power, magically transformed while her lover, watching, exclaims, "You're a Goddess!"

Buffy, by acknowledging Willow as a power that could help her defeat evil, empowered countless women as well as Willow. She also ended her own isolation by reaching out to Willow. If you can, in whatever way possible, even if it's miniscule, acknowledge another woman as a Goddess, you empower her as such and you are no longer alone with *your* burdens, decisions, and sacrifices. And the world can be saved.

Simply be courteous or break through your own biases to try just to listen from the heart, or say to a woman, silently, "You're a Goddess. I don't see why, but I trust it's true." When you do these things, you help a woman find her divinity and then she can stand side by side with you, even if it is in some way you never get to see. Then we're all Goddesses. You're no longer alone. Buffy proposed that after the battle was won, they all go shopping. The mall was mentioned. I love the show's humor, but I prefer online shopping and would love it if you joined me. Next time you save the world—change a diaper, come up with a marketing strategy, write a story, give up your alone time to help a friend or family member, do work you hate because it needs doing—maybe you could get on your computer afterwards. While you're there, credit card ready, know all we Goddesses helped you win the battle and some of us (I'll be there) are out there, somewhere, shopping with you.

how to throw a goddess party

Although this book's games and quizzes can be done almost any time or place—after all, a Goddess is practical!—you can also share one or more of these quizzes and games at a Goddess Party. What an opportunity for deities to convene and combine their infinite and limitless female powers in order to have an immeasurably indulgent time. (Think chocolate.)

How to throw such an event? You're a Goddess! You can do it any way you want. But here are some suggestions.

Make it casual with one or two women over for coffee and donuts. It needn't be more elaborate or planned than that. Just invite them over, ask one of them to bring the pastries, then brew some caffeine, and when they arrive, open this book and let inspiration guide you from there. The moment will take on a life of its own, without any further planning. If, like me, you spend a lot of your food budget in health food stores, change the food and beverage to wheat-free cookies and herbal tea.

If a laid back coffee klatch is not to your taste, make it more elaborate. Plan a pajama party, Goddess style. You can all dress in your pj's, eat popcorn, and do your nails. The game "Presto! Instant Sex Magic!" is perfect pajama party silliness.

Another Goddess party might be more along the lines of your usual party but made special with Goddess-energy. Bestow certificates of Divine Stature on your guests as favors. A Goddess theme might be part of the décor. Don't forget: Goddesses eat chocolate. Honest. Wedding showers and other gatherings take on whole new dimensions when everyone attending is a Goddess!

See "Modern Resources for Modern Goddesses" for more cosmic fun 'n' games to enjoy during parties. And don't forget, these games and quizzes are good entertainment for any sort of event or party, not just for Goddess events.

In any case, as a Goddess, any way you choose to entertain is divine. I won't be hurt if you ignore my suggestions and make up your own way of throwing a Goddess Party. Make it simple and easy, or be creative. But do it! You deserve to.

games
for
goddesses

There's an ancient myth in which some mean old guy-deity tosses an apple along the road thereby somehow causing three Goddesses to chase it and squabble over it. Along with the fact that this myth makes absolutely no sense, that is *not* my idea of a game for Goddesses. The games herein help you not only find your oh-so-divine powers but also celebrate them whether you're alone or with other women, and belly laugh while you're at it!

First, the game instructions, the serious part. "Serious," you ask? Hey, even Scrabble, which I consider a fabulously fun game for erudite Goddesses, has a rule book.

When we dare to be silly, we open to change. Some say it is silly to believe in a better life. So let's be silly. Some say it is foolish to try to love fully and embrace romance. Let's be fools. Some think it's crazy to stand up and make a difference, but others call that brave. In fact, it is fools who find true love, cannily mad rebels who change the world, and silly ideas that make all the difference in our lives and in the lives of those we love.

So the first rule for these games is to open yourself to foolishness, and in doing so open your heart to love, power, change, happiness, and a meaningful life.

The second, and only other, rule, is: Don't worry about doing the games "right." That takes all the fun out of them. Just jump in, figure the games out to the best of your ability—even if that is a befuddled state due to over-consumption of sherry—and have fun!

Helpful info: some games are simpler and shorter than others. The games vary in length of time needed for execution, to suit your needs. For example, at a party, longer games might work better, since a hostess then would not repeatedly have to organize, as well as provide impetus and motivation, to start another game. But on a coffee break with your friends or during a carefree lunch, a quick game with brief text fits the bill.

I tried to create each game so that any type of Goddess would enjoy and benefit from it. Although the games list that appears in each Goddess's chapter shows each game to be especially relevant to three to four deities, every game is fun in its own right, and is truly pertinent to modern women at large, regardless of their "type."

What's most important is that you try the games yourself to discover which you, as an individual, find most fun. (Don't be afraid to actually try a game to see whether or not you like it. Often, that's the only way to know.) What an assignment—to see what you enjoy most!

Once again, and forevermore, let the games begin!

Presto! Instant Sex Magic!

This game is in honor of Marilyn Monroe, the Sex Goddess *par excellence*, and is a bit of entertainment that will soon have you complaining (with a smug smile on your face), "Sigh, I just don't know what to do. Men are following me around, falling into my cleavage, and blushing when I say hello." You need use only some of the following steps if you want.

Step 1. Choose any book. It can be a dictionary, novel, serious political treatise, or the *TV Guide*.

Step 2. Announce, "I am a Sex Goddess." If you're playing this with friends, everyone does each step in turn. After all, if you make a fool of yourself, shouldn't they immediately do so as well, instead of you doing all the steps on your own first? Yes!

Actually, joking aside, I love proclaiming myself a Sex Goddess in a sexy voice. I feel a little silly when I do it, but silly in a good way. Mostly this game just makes me feel confident and happy, not to mention sexy.

Step 3. If you have not already done so, now say "I'm a Sex Goddess" in the sexiest voice possible.

Step 4. Now see if you can say it even sexier, no matter how sexy you may have already said it. You are allowed, nay, *encouraged*, to imitate Suzanne Somers's cute tones, or do a little Marilyn Monroe shimmy after your line has been said; in other words, ham it up!

Step 5. Okay, now make a joke out of it (or more of one if things have already become funny). When you make your announcement, go so over the top with brazen hussiness, sexual bravado, sultry gazes, or coy smugness, that you are the silliest (and cutest) thing since Betty Boop!

Step 6. Now that you've warmed up your vocal libido, read a sentence from the book you chose in step one. Read in the sexiest voice you can come up with. You can intentionally make it humorous if you want.

Step 7. Keep going around the circle (so to speak, since you may not be seated in a circle) with each person in turn reading another line or so. Do as many rounds as you want. When you do several rounds instead of just one, it can get funnier and funnier!

Of course, after I created these games, I test drove each one of them personally, with my friends. There is nothing quite like reading the phone book—"James Smith, 415-888-8888"—each syllable and number sibilant, husky, and dripping with seduction.

The above game is not only fun for anyone who wants to try it, and can obviously bring out the Sex Goddess in you, but can also bring out the Trickster Goddess, Goddess of Love, and Goddess-Just-Wants-to-Have-Fun. Although none of the games need a leader, having one can add more fun. These four Goddesses are likely candidates to lead the game.

The "I Can't Hear You" Game

There are some expressions we Modern Goddesses simply have no patience for. Such as "Did you put on a few extra pounds?" And "Why would *you* need a raise?" Or "If you were able to get a nice man, maybe you wouldn't be so concerned about political change (or your career, or spirituality...)." Or "Why don't you smile?" And "What's the big problem, anyway? Don't overreact so much." Or how about "Don't bother. What's the point? Nothing you do'll make a difference anyway." Or "Be realistic. You'll never be able to pull *that* off." Argh! I can't stand it!

This game shows you how to deal with such drivel. After all, you're a Goddess. You don't have to put up with this nonsense!

Step 1. Think of a remark *you* hate to hear and that a person or people keep repeating to you. Or, instead, did anyone say anything particularly annoying, infuriating, or frustrating to you today?

Step 2. Write one remark down.

Step 3. Then say, as if addressing the person(s) who made the comment, "I can't *hear* you!" If you're doing this with others, it's sometimes easier to make your proclamation if everyone says it aloud with you, simultaneously, perhaps on the count of three. "One, two, three, I can't *hear* you!" This way you're free of embarrassment, should it be hard for you to hear the sound of your own voice fighting back loudly against rude remarks when others are present. Besides, doing it as an ensemble, you're all likely to fall over laughing!

Step 4. If making your rebuttal wasn't as fulfilling as butter-pecan ice cream, then say it again, but this time louder and more vehemently. Or say it again for the same reason you have more ice cream—because it feels good.

In fact, you may want to recite your line repeatedly—"Again! One, two, three, I can't hear you!"—three to ten times, perhaps becoming louder and more vehement with each repetition. As you repeat this phrase three things can happen:

You can laugh more and more with delight at your rebellion and the foolishness of the game.

You may find you're blowing off steam about the absurd remark you're refuting, until its inanity holds less power over you.

You may work up the gumption not to take such oblivious input lying down.

Then, the next time someone says something so stupid you can't believe it, you might be more able to talk to that person about it, or in the quiet of your own mind to announce, "I can't *hear* you!" as you politely and pleasantly nod to them as if their words actually made sense!

Feel free, when playing the game, to make your declaration silently. It's probably better to say it out loud, but if the only way you can do it is in your head, go for it. Repeat it, internally, imagining your voice becoming louder and more vehement each time. You'll still likely enjoy the game and gain its benefits.

Step 5. When in a group, take turns, each woman starting with Step 1, addressing one remark she hates, as many times as she needs (in other words, going through all the steps) then another woman doing the same, until everyone's had a chance.

Step 6. If you choose, go another round. Start the game all over again—with a new objectionable remark for each participant—for more fun, power, effectiveness, laughter, and tomfoolery.

Step 7. Whether alone or with friends, go as many rounds as you choose until the steam runs out and you're ready to conquer the world.

Then go conquer it!

The Big Secret

My mother used to say, about making your way through life, "Always be a lady. If nothing else, it'll drive them crazy."

I like to think that was her little, secret weapon and she knew she could always rely on it. If nothing else, she could drive them crazy, and likely get her way. Or at least escape with minimum losses!

Every Goddess needs a secret, one that gives her a Mona Lisa smile. One that makes her feel oh-so-smug, and that she can fall back on when she enters a room.

Having said that, the game is simple. You can play it any time, anywhere. You just say to yourself, "I have a secret." Mind you, you may not know what the secret is at that moment. The important thing is that you imagine you have one and that you pretend to yourself it's a really big magic-weapon-super-power through which you always come out on top. That's the game: to pretend. There's no more to it than that! But it is great, because it, well, it's like when you were little and pretended to be a princess or movie star: the world is yours!

If you happen to figure out in the middle of the game what your secret actually is, that's an added bonus! Maybe your secret is your knowledge that with God(dess) in your life everything works out in the long run. Or simply that you *know absolutely* how fabulous you look today. Your secret may be different each time you play the game.

Helpful hint: You may want to pretend *you have no doubt* that this secret weapon exists. Imagine within yourself the peace and satisfaction that this confidence brings. Hold that feeling for a few minutes if you can. No matter *how* much you want to tell yourself otherwise, you do have many secret weapons, and if you imagine that to be true, they may no longer be secrets to *you*.

How to Be (at Least a Bit of) a Bad Girl Goddess, Version #1

I had so much fun thinking up ways to be bad that I came up with two versions of this game. Here's the first:

The Train Wreck Boogie

Select any melody you know. It can be a rock tune, a country and western song, a ballad, or anything else. It doesn't matter if you know the melody well. Sing the words below to it. They won't fit! Or they likely won't fit. And that is good because it will make things goofy. (Thus the lyrics will get to sneak by your ever-alert Good Girl Goddess and sink into your unconscious mind, thereby programming you to release the impish, mischievous Cosmic Bitch Within.)

Don't sit down and actually try to set the lyrics to the tune, note for note. Just improvise and let things happen as they will.

When a performance of a song ends up a total mess, perhaps even stopping dead on the track, musicians call it a "train wreck." A train wreck is almost guaranteed to happen with this game, so don't fuss or worry. Just do what the musical pros do—enjoy finishing out the song in some way, shape, or form. The goal is not musical excellence. It is, remember, the devious programming of your subconscious mind.

Lyrics:

I'm bad and that's good.
I'm the worst bitch in the
   neighborhood.
Anything I shouldn't do
is my goal and is my due.

I'm bad and that's fun.
I can take on anyone.
Give me trouble
and you better run.

(I didn't say these were genius lyrics, but they get the job done.)

I'm bad all the while.
I'll seduce you with a smile.
Anything that this gal wants
comes her way, ready or not!

After composing this masterpiece I tried singing it to the tune of The Beatles' "I Saw Her Standing There." I had to skip over some lines of melody, and, all in all, it was a mess. And that was part of what made it fun!

I also tried singing it to the tune of "Jingle Bells." If my neighbors had peeked in my window and seen me doing that, they probably would have called the men in white coats, who would have come and taken me away. It would have been worth it!

My Bad Girl Goddess dream is someday to be walking down the street and see little girls playing, happily and free, their darling pigtails bouncing up and down as they skip rope reciting in their innocent, childlike sing-song "I'm bad and that's fun. I can take on anyone."

Hee, hee, hee.

Reminders: As is the case with all the games, "The Train Wreck Boogie" is for *anyone*. However, Bad Girl, Girlfriend, Trickster, and Sex Goddesses can be particularly effective in leading it. Though none of these games need a leader, having one can always help create more merriment.

How to Be (at Least a Bit of) a Bad Girl Goddess, Version #2

Version #2 is a brief, to-the-point and to-the-punch lesson in the "F*** You Smile," known to waitresses throughout the country. One smiles ever so nicely, while thinking, "F*** you." Thus has the sanity and sense of humor of women in service positions been repeatedly saved ever since this game was first invented. That's it, that's all there is to it, that's the total game. But airline stewardesses, nurses, administrative assistants, store clerks, and the like all need this game. Wicked fun!

No one who lives in L.A. is allowed to play this game. You who reside in the realm of film, flash, and big deals already have too many subtle, courteous ways of saying "F*** you."

I want to make it clear that the author of this book would never play this game. So if you run into her and you are being a bit difficult, and she becomes oh-so-pleasant-and-nice, with the sincerest, most polite smile on her face, she is simply demonstrating her compassion for your trials, and accepting you despite your shortcomings. Honest.

I love making up games. I also love getting credit for what I do. But I can't take credit for this game; it was taught to me by a bartender. I did not work at that bar. So I never used the game. Honest.

Bless Your Secret Magic Weapon

This game instills self-confidence as you learn to use a piece of jewelry—it can be one you already own—as a touchstone of assuredness.

Everyone participating brings a piece of jewelry. This could be anything a person chooses for herself—a ring you already wear every day, a pin you save for dates, or a new necklace bought just for the game.

Next, acquire Fairy dust. Find some flour or rosemary from your kitchen cupboard. Or use glitter. Whatever you use, it is *your* Fairy dust, because I say it is. Ha!

Each participant takes a fingerfull of Fairy dust, sprinkles it over her secret magic weapon—her piece of jewelry—then says, "When I wear this and say the magic word, I am (fill in the blank with one word, for example: confident, brave, sexy, cheerful, humorous, focused, independent, effective, insightful)."

Then whenever you want to activate your magic weapon, say the magic word—it is whatever word you used to fill in the blank—and put the piece of jewelry on. You will now have the stated attribute while wearing the jewelry.

Here's where foolishness comes in handy: be willing to feel silly enough to believe doing the game might actually help you feel better. Even if it only works a bit, I believe that in itself is very good.

Here's an example from my own life. (I use myself as an example because if I can pull something off, *anyone* can. Forget following some all-knowing oh-great-one. Walk next to fumbling-oh-me, and together we'll achieve the great things we hope to.)

I have an album of music that I produced myself, with the budget of a grocery list! Furthermore, I had no experience in music studios, distribution, or any other part of the nuts and bolts of the process except the actual music making. The album received wonderful reviews, is distributed internationally, and, best of all, people I don't know write to me saying they really enjoy it. I had to take a series of the tiniest steps to make the album happen. In fact, it took ten years of false starts before I finally got into a music studio to start recording. After each tiny step, whether fruit came from it or not, I took another. If health—I've dealt with a lot of physical disabilities in my life—or something else stopped my progress entirely, I eventually got back to my tiny steps.

Finally, enough ground had been covered, momentum built, abilities gained, that big steps could happen.

Just a little pinch of Fairy dust!

Having said that the game may only help a little, I'll add that just as often I've seen something like this help a lot!

Princess Pink Day

Princess Pink Day is day-long fun during which you (and anyone you want to join you, if you regally *deign* to let someone join you) get to drink pink (Kool-Aid!), think pink, and all in all, indulge pink. In other words, you spend the day involved in frivolities of all sorts. Perfect for Sunday brunch cum an afternoon with friends.

Do your day as elaborately or as minimally as you want. If exquisite details float your boat, go high style. If a lazy day seems more regal, keep this simple and easy. Here are some suggestions for Princess Pink Day. Feel free to vary them or toss them out and substitute your own pink pleasures.

First, food. My personal recipe: Fairy Princess Grapes. Buy pink sugar—the type for decorating confections—and red grapes. Use scissors to cut the grapes into little bunches of two to six grapes, which makes easy handling for your guests. Then roll each bunch in the sugar and stack them all in a pink crystal or pink plastic (or any other color or material) bowl. My friend Phoebe says this recipe is ditzy, but we agreed that that's a good thing and makes Fairy Princess Grapes work. Let's face it, royalty *is* ditzy, and that's why Princess Pink Day is wonderful.

More pink foods, as well as beverages:

* Raspberry Kool-Aid
* Bubbly mineral water with a few raspberries dropped in as visual accents
* Watermelon
* Packaged cake mix
* Packaged frosting anointing store-bought cookies
* Strawberry ice cream
* Cherry yogurt
* Pink grapefruit

Petit fours, no matter the color, are perfect, because of their sheer and delicate extravagance.

I would suggest pureeing watermelon in a blender, after which you pour it over ice for a delectable beverage but, honestly, I don't know if it would be good or not! Or if it would even *be a beverage*. Maybe it would just end up as tasteless slush. Hmm, maybe if you added some white grape juice, sugar and...okay, this is not a cookbook, and I'm not qualified to write one (though I think my grape idea quite nice), but you may want to experiment with watermelon.

As for the decor for the big day, look through your home: you may have pink on hand already. Easter decorations? Ribbons to tie around baskets or candlesticks, or drape along the walls? A pink-haired troll doll sitting in a planter, and *voilà*, a centerpiece! One or two items of decoration are enough to set the tone, so don't feel obliged to make a big deal out of it unless you get the urge.

Fresh or fake flowers can make you feel pampered.

Want to be really princessy? Go on a shopping spree and buy a lot of items, from food to decor to clothing, to use on Princess Pink Day. Or purchase one special treat for yourself—perhaps a cut crystal bowl that, while not pink, might look fabulous holding the Fairy Princess Grapes.

If you're preparing a brunch or other full meal, don't be rigid about all edibles being you-know-what-color. This is supposed to be a pleasure, not an exercise in neurosis! A few foods colored for Princess Pink Day set the tone. I mean, food coloring in mashed potatoes? Ew, that's nauseating!

A potluck might make this brunch less work for one person.

Party favors: tiaras with exquisite rhinestones are my first choice. But if your budget is not up to that, look for a party or stationery store that has party hats in the shape of little crowns and tiaras. Pink Mardi Gras beads and other party trappings, including crowns and tiaras, can be found in the Oriental Trading Company's catalog. Goddesses should know about this publication anyway: it is chock-full of magnificent party favors, costumes to embody your cosmic powers, colorful decorations that range from the grand to the ridiculous, gimmick pencils, seasonal chachkas to celebrate your divine passage through your divine year, and more. They're listed in the resource guide at the end of the book.

Other favors (suitably colored, of course) include: a carnation for each guest; a bottle of glittery nail polish; and lip gloss. Haunt your local mall or chain drugstore for teens' accoutrements. They can be quite inexpensive and nobody knows how to princess like a teenager: floral decals to wear on nails; plastic gem bracelets that glimmer and glisten; glittery eyeshadow. Even if the color is not you-know-which-one, if it feels like luxury or fun, get it! Anything with glitter or fake gems strikes a princess chord—frivolous, fantasy, and fabulous.

Since Princess Pink Day constitutes the act of loving yourself up, there is a special party favor that's perfect: rose quartz. An inexpensive pink crystal, it is known in metaphysical circles as the stone of self-love. A single rose quartz bead on a string, worn as a necklace, or a tiny, rough chunk of it tucked into a pouch and hung about the neck is reputed to help one gain self-love. You can also find beautiful and inexpensive rose quartz jewelry.

Don't refrain from doing a solitary Princess Pink Day. You might think you won't enjoy it alone or that it is not worth the effort. I beg you, beg you, beg you, do it! There's something about preparing Fairy Princess Grapes for yourself that touches you deep within—the little eight-year-old girl inside you who wants a pink party dress and tiara can be fulfilled by a solitary Princess Pink Day, or even part of one. And every Goddess should at least once have the experience of wearing a crown all day long in the lunatic and delightful solitude of her own home! Here are some other ideas suitable to do on your own, instead of or along with any of the suggestions above:

* Look in a drugstore for a little girl's bubble bath in you-know-what color.
* Buy matching towels and enjoy a spa-like experience. Heck, buy matching sheets to retire in at day's end.

* How about body lotion, nightie, and rhinestone barrettes, all in pink for when you emerge from the tub?
* How about splurging on a high-end cologne that for some reason smells that color to you?

Alone or with friends, activities might include:

* Painting nails. There's such a range of colors nowadays, that *some* color pink would suit everyone.
* Facial masques of any color are regal treatment.
* Gossip. It's one of life pleasures, so I'll include it without any other justification. And a princess has to do *something* with all her leisure time! If you're alone, make a long-neglected phone call to catch up with a distant friend.

Feel free to throw out my guidelines and make up your own way of executing Princess Pink Day. The important thing is, this game is about indulgence and, um, pink and, of course, silliness.

Enjoy!

Cosmic Coincidence Used for Fortune Telling

This activity provides not only a bit of laughter but perhaps some guidance. Like the book's other briefer games, it is a perfect respite during a coffee break when your work day has been frazzling. At the end of the day, when you're also at the end of your wits, exhausted, this game can also be a quick, easy pick-me-up.

Sometimes when someone is puzzled and needs guidance, I suggest she open up a book to a random page—any book, even a cookbook—and let her eyes fall on whatever sentence they happen to fall on. I ask her to read the sentence to see if those words have meaning for her. This exercise might make more sense to some folks if they are using the Bible, or another spiritual text, but the point is that the universe provides us guidance in the strangest ways and we need to be open to it. A bit of foolishness opens us up to that guidance.

Do this alone or get together with friends and let everyone take a turn, first asking a question of the cosmos, then opening the book and seeing what the answer is. You may not learn anything, but you will at least laugh—after all, this is a game. And you may be amazed to find some real insights!

By the way, I find it interesting that I am not the only person who thought of this game. I've met other people who use this technique for guidance. There are universal experiences, and among them is a trickster element, influencing how divine guidance comes to us.

Cosmic Coincidental Fortune Telling Stories

That's a mouthful, and fun to write.

In this game, a person or group uses randomly chosen excerpts from books to weave a nonsense story that not only evokes grand silliness but might also reveal the future!

Everyone should first get a book to refer to. Then the group tells a story in the following way: (You can do this on your own by gathering up several books and going from one to another, in random order.)

Step 1. After everyone is gathered in a circle, each person says out loud or to themselves what they are hoping for guidance about.

Remember, this is a game. Whatever it is you want guidance about should be something light. There are other times you can be, and need to be, more serious about your healing work. This book is about learning to heal through fun!

Step 2. The first person opens to a page at random and reads a line. It can be a full sentence or a phrase.

Step 3. The next person in the circle opens to a page at random and chooses another line (which can be a full sentence or a phrase). Before stating the chosen line, you may want to use one of the following words to connect it to the previous line, so that we start a story.

- and
- then
- but
- nevertheless
- or
- until
- finally

For example, if the first person's line is "Baste the chicken every few minutes," the second person might use the word "then" to preface her line "hold him tight and never let him go." The result: "Baste the chicken every few minutes, then hold him tight and never let him go."

Sometimes a connective word or phrase will be unnecessary. The participants get a sense of story anyway—all the funnier for its utter lack of continuity. And don't worry! Thinking about which connective word to use may slow things down too much sometimes. Let the word come to you easily or don't use one. If you like, use a word not listed here, or make up a whole connective *phrase* if inspiration hits and one just comes to you: "Baste the chicken every few minutes, *then be true to yourself and* hold him tight and never let him go." The important thing here is just relaxing and randomly choosing your line so that the story can flow in its incoherent, yet often surprisingly coherent manner. With that flow comes the just-as-important flow of laughter.

Step 4. Continue around the circle, each person adding a new phrase or sentence, preceding the addition with a connective word or phrase.

Cheating is allowed. If, when randomly choosing text from your book, you find you don't want to use it, whatever the reason, flip to another page. Or, again, make up your own connecting phrases, if that would be even more fun than the ones I provide.

Don't get too fastidious about the story's grammar, either. It may not always work, and sometimes things will be gibberish, but that is part of the fun. As I said, if you try too hard to figure out which connecting word works best, you'll spoil the spontaneity. So it is with the game as a whole: make relaxed fun the priority.

Step 5. Repeatedly go around the circle, everyone taking turns adding new randomly chosen lines. A sense of story may bit by bit emerge that might strike a chord for you regarding the question you brought to this game. However, in the same way that the story is likely to amount to nonsense, so the guidance that accompanies the tale might at times be unclear.

Don't expect a message to be spelled out for you. While it may happen, the story might instead hold the *sense* of an idea you need or the hint of a direction your life needs to go or another non-linear and not so clear bit of help. Play around with whatever you get in order to derive advice from it.

This is actually the point of the game: Instead of receiving guidance through a logical process, you play by creating a story, then interpret the guidance from the story in the same manner. Thus you might arrive at valuable insights that you could not achieve through brow-furrowing, overly serious logic and brain-tiring work.

Ancient Taoists taught us that a relaxed smile, coupled with an acceptance of randomness—and here I am not referring to the randomness of the story, but to the way people participate in the game—open us up to all the powers of the universe, which are then at our disposal. If you instead set about this, or any of the games, grimly, frantic about whether or not you perform each detail absolutely correctly, you close down to the cosmos's wonders. Thus, in this particular game, by relaxing and enjoying yourself, you're likely to receive some real guidance from the cosmically coincidental story.

A last note: If no insight comes during the course of the game, it may arrive later. As I said earlier, when we open up to the trickster element, we open up to guidance. I also said, just above here, that relaxed fun embodies the Taoist approach to life. Once you've played this game, you've opened up for a bit. Insights can then come to you, even if they don't arrive immediately. Look for them in yet more random places. A thought that pops into your head, words on the back of a cereal box, a picture on the side of a bus! Never let it be said that God(dess) does not have a sense of humor when it comes to offering us advice.

Love, Love, and More Love

Here is more productive foolishness:

We're about to do an imitation of Shakespeare's three witches and their "Double, double, toil and trouble." Making fun of these outrageous characters almost always causes me to chortle. But the way this game is played, we'll in truth be affirming love in all its forms, whether world peace or romance, and thus helping open our hearts and lives to love, love, and more love. And because we're *modern* Goddesses, we get to use a cup of tea or coffee as the magical cauldron.

A game about love, in the most inclusive sense of the word, is the perfect finale for this book because the power of all Goddesses, all women, is essentially love. And to honor *l'amour*, and end our journey with a magnificent, womanly flourish, this'll be one of the book's long games, done with luscious depth and intricacy. Each of the book's modern Goddesses is honored in this game—a big ending with a lot of fanfare! The game itself is in honor of the Love Goddess. And using the three evil crones—Bad Girl Goddess all the way.

If you are a witch, I hope this parody doesn't offend you. Witchcraft, often called Wicca, is a legitimate, ethical religion that demonstrates meaningful depth, caring, and ability to help change the world. One of the strengths Wicca brings to the interfaith community is the ability to laugh at oneself. If more spiritual groups had a sense of humor about themselves, there would be far less pomposity and far more compassion. The witches I know love to do take-offs on Shakespeare's three gals.

Step 1. Brew yourself a yummy beverage. Coffee, chicken soup, an ice cream soda, herbal tea, a bowl of partially-melted ice cream (don't you love it when it gets a bit soft like that?), diet cola, beer, wine, whatever. I know one does not *brew* ice-cream sodas nor some of the other items I just listed. Nor is a bowl of ice cream a beverage. If you're a person who slavishly nit-picks about that sort of thing, get over it!

In the same vein, I am not suggesting you brew your own beer or wine. Unless you want to. Instead, pour it into a glass. Dump the ice cream or ice cream sodas into appropriate containers. Ditto *whatever* your drink of choice for this game will be.

Step 2. Find something you can stir your drink with when you get to that part of the game. (If you put completely frozen ice cream in a dish, by the time we get to it, it might have softened a bit. Then, when you stir it in the game, you'll be getting it all soft and mushy and perfect.)

Now that we have all our ducks lined up, we are ready to start our version of Shakespeare's magical spell.

Step 3. Witch or not, deep down every woman has magic. The real word for magic is *love*.

You can call what you believe in Wicca, Christianity, Buddhism, or simple human decency, but it all comes down to love. And lest you think I'm on a tangent here, this all circles round to the matter at hand. Because, of course, this game is *about love*. Tangent proven relevant = homage to Trickster Goddess in this game.

In fact, I think of this game as a *comedic interfaith prayer*. Some Trickster Goddesses pray, and whomever they pray to has a sense of humor. All deities do. If in some small way what we're about to do is an act of love from the heart, then it becomes a prayer of sorts. Sincere love is prayer as much as love is magic. And what a Christian defines as a prayer, a non-religious person might call an affirmation, a Wiccan a spell, a mystic the act of connecting the cosmic dots in order to weave a net that holds all things in blessing, a Native American Shaman...

Shakespeare's three hags didn't really understand magic. A lot of people don't. They think it is about controlling others, hexing, evil, or a big, dark, dirty secret. Here is the real secret of magic: We create enchantment with the magic in our own hearts and souls. A great piece of art is magic because it lifts our spirits. A sincere poem is magic because it makes us feel less alone. It is magic when you hug your child, because in doing so you help him or her feel safe and cared for. Magic is a sunrise, a fully open rose, a fully open heart.

You know, "the magic of cinema" as they say. "A magic moment" when lovers meet. "The magic of your smile" as the song says. So, we honor the New Age Goddess in this game—her for whom love and wonder and mysticism go hand in hand all day long—and the Girlfriend Goddess whose down-to-earth caring is an ongoing spell creating happiness for those she loves.

What is the real secret of love? Foolishness. When we open to foolishness, we open to love because love is a game fools ultimately win. So we'll be silly in this game. We'll make our wish for love by offering up our foolishness. It's sacred foolishness because in it we find hope and dreams. Thus we pay homage to the starry-eyed Out-to-Change-the-World-Goddess, with her idealism and simple faith that everything always turns out for the best.

Now, on to the game/spell/prayer/affirmation/lunacy:

This game is a very ancient practice. (I swear.)

Placing your beverage (or ice cream) in front of you, along with whatever you're going to stir it with, close your eyes, and try to look as pompous as possible.

Step 4. If you're playing with friends, now peek at each other to see how foolish you all appear. Whether you're doing this alone or not, open your eyes anyway, to read the next instructions.

Step 5. With all the grand gestures and over-inflated pomp and ceremony you can muster, start stirring your cauldron. If you totally lack any flair for the dramatic, just stir. And try not to feel too stupid. Or, honor the Sex Goddess, by stirring as sensuously as possible. Or invoke the Goddess of Wrath and Unintentional Destruction, with clumsy gestures. (Goddess-Just-Wants-To-Have-Fun, this and the following goofiness is tailored to you and your willingness to try out new, fun ideas!)

Step 6. Stir for at least a full two or three minutes, perhaps making mystical mumbling sounds, lifting your nose high in the air as if you were the High-Muckity-Muck-Priestess-of-All-Magical-Realms, and/or trying to look very wise and deep. This step is perfect for Princess Goddess.

Step 7. Now we move to Shakespeare's chant—which I have revised. I'm sorry to blemish the great bard's work, but "Double, double, toil and trouble" is so negative! And the part earlier where they say "thrice the brindled cat hath mewed, thrice and once the hedge pig whined"? That's not relevant to a modern Goddess, nor is it that decipherable.

When I looked at the whole, long chant he wrote, I threw most of it out. It's filled with icky ingredients that you're supposed to throw into the pot, and some other parts of the chant are abysmal. I know the Corporate Goddess would say, "It's not good marketing to use such unappealing text." So, in honor of the Corporate Goddess, who knows how to take any idea and make it more practical, you'll find my modern version following. Recite it with all the foolish pomp, laughter, and absurdity you've thus far mustered. Or at least recite it.

Remember, this is an affirmation of love for us all, love for the world, love for those who are most in need. Think of love in the broadest sense, that of compassion and respect for others. Think of justice, and food and shelter, and peace and dignity. These things honor the Activist Goddess. You can also consider this game a prayer/wish/affirmation/spell/whatever-you-want-to-call-it for romance. I don't know about you, but I want a date.

Chorus
Double, double, free of trouble,
fire burn and cauldron bubble.
[This second line *is* Shakespeare's.]

Verse
Fill the pot with tea or grog,
ice cream, soda, or eggnog,
any drink or food not odd,
no eye of newt or toe of frog.
["Eye of newt and toe of frog" are in the original. Blech.]

Repeat Chorus

Fill the pot with hope and cheer,
kind of like if Yule-tide's here.
[Yup, this is dumb. It should be.]
Not just pots but people, too,
here's the wish I make for you:

Repeat Chorus

May true love be everywhere—
under, over, there, and here.
May all hearts be filled with smiles
so that humankind is free.

I couldn't get those last two lines to rhyme. I don't care. Because my devious plan is as follows: I hope that performing all the silliness that preceded those lines will have, as I said earlier, opened our hearts to a bit more hope for a better life for ourselves and a better world for everyone else. So, ideally, we're past the point of needing the rhyme, and can end this game, and this book, on a serious note:

Step 8. Though the game is complete with what we have already done, those of you who want to continue in order to do even more to make a better world, please go on with me, in one last step.

Below is a straight ahead prayer for love. And what better way to pray/affirm/wish/etc. for love than to do so in a way that honors all religions? (I respect all religions, except those that do not respect all *other* religions. In fact, I also respect people's choice to *avoid* religion.) Religious bigotry, even though it's often based in misunderstandings about spiritual practices that are different from one's own, have been one of the greatest causes of poverty, misery, and war.

I am someone who practices the Wiccan religion, as well as the ancient Chinese religion, Taoism, and who also has a relationship with Christ. Recently, my personal struggles have also led me to create spiritual practices for myself that I'm realizing are typical of Buddhism, *and* I spiritually counsel and teach people of all religions, I'm an interfaith community unto myself! So, I think I'm suited for the job of leading an interfaith blessing.

Picture me, if you like, leading you in this prayer, as the Good Fairy of Self-Help—Fairy wings, pink and blue hair, sparkling with fairy dust head to toe, wearing striped munchkin stockings.

Some people who believe in something divine and more powerful than themselves call it God, others call it Goddess. Others think of it as a nameless creator or Great Eagle, or a flow of goodness in the universe. Others have yet another way to view it. On the next page is a prayer for love. Since I pray to my Divine Mom and Dad, I use their names in the prayer. This is also a way for this last game to honor you who embody the Mother Goddess. But you who believe in something else, please substitute your name(s) for it. If you don't believe in a greater being, adapt the prayer in whatever way is right for you. Make it into an affirmation, for example, or a statement of your commitment to create love in the world and in your own life.

I thank *you*—all who are playing this game—for joining with me in creating love and for enjoying this book with me so that we all can help others and have great sex!

And now I will go out into the world, as I hope you will do, to find the phone numbers of fabulous lovers, while I try to create world peace.

But wait. If you want suggestions as to where you can go from here, read on.

"Great Mother Goddess and
    your Boyfriend,
our Good Father Whom we need not fear,
bless us so that
we can create love.

Mother Father God,
Please bless those who are most in need.
Bless us all here.
Bless this planet,
that all people and beings everywhere,
    myself included, find love.

Thank you Mother and Father for
    your blessings.
Please help me live them in my daily life.
So be it."

modern
resources
for modern
goddesses

Below are additional goodies for Goddesses, so that you keep growing into your Godhood as much and for as long as you want.

Don't expect the stuffy, boring artifacts and activities sought after by wanna-be Goddesses of generations past. From glamour and glitz to the more serious end of the spectrum, herein is the *real* stuff—instead of magic wands you'll find magic makeup; instead of obscure chants you can have spiritual rock 'n' roll.

The modern Goddess is not a deluded neurotic wearing a cape! (Well, *I'm* a deluded neurotic wearing a cape, but not all my divine sisters are.) So here are products and services to further support your fabulously hip, modern divinity:

❋ Check out yoficosmetics.com. Whether they know it or not, they're a Goddess resource, what with a zillion colors of cosmetic grade glitters. Some Goddesses just don't feel right without pink glitter on lips and eyes! (That would be me.)

❋ All Goddesses know how to phone-chat, so *all* you need is your phone for Telephone-Goddess games. Join me for a quick 'n' snappy lunch hour or evening Goddess game. For more info about this and any other services and products below that are offered by *moi*, I can be reached at 415-750-1205; P.O. Box 210307, San Francisco, CA 94121.

✳ Or contact me via *The Wiccan & Faerie Grimoire of Francesca De Grandis* at www.well.com/user/zthirdrd/WiccanMiscellany.html, which is a resource in itself. It has rituals, spells, articles and other Goddess writings, mostly serious, some silly. You'll also find instructions there for how to be on my e-mailing list to receive helpful spiritual hints via my free newsletters, and news of upcoming books, classes, and other events.

✳ You'll notice a theme in this resource guide—the telephone! Both that and the computer can be as important to the modern female deity as springing forth from the ocean naked on a giant clam shell was for the ancient Goddess of Love, Aphrodite.

So, I searched out a cute phone and found "The Swedish Royal Family Reproduction Telephone," absurdly, wonderfully ornate, looking like it belongs in your cosmic castle. I found it at Toscano Design, 800-525-0733 or DesignToscano.com. Ask for item #pm-1893.

A woman's environment should honor her power, beauty, and wisdom. Telephone aside, Toscano Design is great for gracing your temple—aka your home, office, garden, etc.—with styles fit for your divine stature. Toscano specializes in historical reproductions that are fab indoors and out. Along with the phone, I noted fountains, sculptures, jewelry, furniture, wall décor, to name only a few categories.

A Goddess needn't be blatant in creating a suitable environment for herself. If a woman decorates her person and surroundings with care, self-respect, and perhaps a bit of glamour and mischief, she's automatically adorning herself as a Goddess and creating a setting in which she can shine as such. Others might not be able to quite put their finger on what that particular shine is, and why it's so appealing, but the glow will still draw them, hold them, and keep them happy.

Ancient Goddesses often walked disguised amidst humankind. We have license to do the same. Our counterparts of old walked on the earth pretending to be human. They were able to create all sorts of fabulous mischief, seduce dreamboats who caught their eye, and thoroughly celebrate earthly pleasures. They used all their power, beauty, and allure, even though others were not consciously aware that these Goddesses *were* Goddesses. So we too, if we desire, can pretend to be mere mortals, and take secret advantage of our superhuman prowess.

Toscano, and many of the other suppliers in this guide, may not consider themselves resources for Goddesses. But we know better. In the case of Toscano, they offer items that can supply suitable grandeur, imagination, and opulence.

✳ In the same vein, I wonder if the Oriental Trading Company, at 800-228-2269, knows how often their number is dialed by contemporary divinities. Call them for their catalog. Mentioned earlier in this book, this company is truly worth looking into—they've a bizarrely free-ranging line of offerings that seems without theme, which means their products will suit a wide variety of Goddesses. If there *is* a theme, it's their low prices, on everything from stick-on body gems to stuff to entertain the kids while you're trying to stick *on* your body gems. They even carry wedding favors, hula skirts, and arts 'n' craft supplies. You name it...

Tell Oriental Trading Company I sent you. No, I don't have an arrangement with them, but maybe if they come to recognize my name as someone who supports them, they'll forgive me for my constant phone calls during which I ask annoying questions like "Now, *exactly* what color is that papier-mâché donkey that you're selling?"

Tell any of the vendors in this chapter I sent you. I have no special deal with any of them, but perhaps those of them with whom I have done business will forgive me my sins, considering how long I've kept some of them on the phone.

A serious note about this chapter: I am simply sharing my personal opinion about resources I have enjoyed myself, or turning you on to something that I haven't used but which looks like it might be cool. I am not vouching for anything saying, for example, it is trouble free, or that the vendor in question is someone I know and who has impeccable ethics. This guide is just girlfriend chat. So *you* need to decide whether to use a resource or not; it's your responsibility if it doesn't work out well. Okay, sister Goddess, now that I've made it clear I'm not Ms. Codependent Goddess, let's rock 'n' roll: onto more resources.

✳ Despite my earlier wisecrack about magic wands, I have one. It tunes me in to my psychic skills, and helps me focus on my spiritual nature, as do incenses and other ritual accoutrements. Such items are fun but also enhance the serious part of my Goddess quest. Two sources are http://store.stormsong.org/ and http://www.moonlightmysteries.com

✳ As for those of us who want to run about in capes and gothic skirts with lace blouses that have huge ruffled cuffs (and our hair half-way down our backs), Gypsy Moon is the high-end way to go. Velvets creamy to the touch, diaphanous silks, draping fabrics—this is the stuff that makes other women seriously jealous! I put on one of their outfits, looked in the mirror, and felt *gorgeous*. Like a woman in a Pre-Raphaelite painting, dreamy, soft, feminine, in layers of almost sheer, muted silks.

Not that I can wear all this stuff grocery shopping, but a lot of the line is street wear, and it's all thoroughly girly and romantic: www.gypsymoon.com, or call 617-876-7095.

✳ A Goddess can tune in to the cosmic airwaves for advice and power. And when she can't, she *calls* me! (One reason I love phones: they're a direct link to the divine sisterhood.) I provide spiritual counseling by telephone for Goddesses and Gods all over the world. Appointments are suitable for people of any religion or lack thereof. I treat you as an individual so you receive what *you* need.

For example, you can learn more about being a woman who controls her life and follows her star. Perhaps you want to heal your internal blocks to a Goddess's power, inner wisdom, and capacity to be there for others. Or maybe you need to solve problems. If a few have developed because you're trying to attain personal growth and confidence—you might even hit such a snag while using this book—or you need input and peace of mind so you can be decisive about love, family, or career, I'd love to help.

Go for a one-on-one telephone appointment or a Goddess party phone call. With the latter, I'm your party-psychic, with mini-readings for you and your friends. La, la, la, easy entertainment and full-tilt girl giggles.

✳ If you need a counselor, but don't think I'm the person you need, don't stop there. Keep looking. Look for someone you can trust or whom you are at least willing to trust a little so that you can find out whether you can trust them enough. Use common sense and, maybe, intuition, making sure you choose the right person not only in terms of whether they are up to snuff but whether they have expertise in what you need to discuss. Maybe a friend knows someone.

Don't desperately accept the first person who appears. When you're upset or vulnerable, it's easy to do so. But during a crisis, it's all the more important you take some time to determine if a counselor is right for you, and, if not, move on to look some more. You can interview most people to see if you want to work with them. Or at least do a test session and evaluate from there.

When you're upset and pressed, it can be hard to trust your own judgment. Run your impressions and thoughts about a possible counselor by a friend to get feedback.

If you are struggling with difficult emotions, feel stuck in your life, or are challenged by a past or present trauma, you can overcome your problems with a counselor who works in a psychologically-based treatment mode, or one who works spiritually. I would be honored to be of service to you as the latter, but if I'm not right for you or you're not in the San Francisco Bay Area and don't want to try phone counseling, I repeat: please look for another spiritual healer, psychic, pastoral counselor, or minister in your own neck of the woods.

Get help if you need it. Do what it takes to get it.

✻ Moving on: if you want to explore Goddess Spirituality as a serious religious path you can attend my San Francisco Bay Area classes, or enjoy the training where you live: I teach tele-seminars—classes by telephone. Again, you only need your phone. I love 'em.

✻ The CD, *Pick the Apple from the Tree,* is a collection of Goddess Spirituality music that ranges from religious parody to divine rock to sexy siren song. Phone Serpentine Music at 800-270-5009 to order, or go to my site at www.well.com/user/zthirdrd/sacredtoys.html where there's more fun Goddess paraphernalia.

✻ Good Vibrations, at www.goodvibes.com, is a woman-owned company that offers erotic toys and sex education. Forget the sleazy establishments where nervous people furtively shop. Good Vibrations is wholesome, upbeat, and feminist. Need I add fun? If you make it to San Francisco, a visit to their shop should be on your agenda. It's a sweet store. I mean, I went there to attend an art opening of erotic photography. Get the idea?

✳ When gathering these resources, I asked Girlfriend Goddess Jane Lind for ideas. She suggested Good Vibrations, which elicited a "Duh! Of course" from me. Which brings me to another resource—your fellow Goddesses. As you continue your trek toward full divinity, don't forget to ask them for ideas or where to find what you need. Jane's cosmetic and skin-care findings, which you'll see below, are useful to me not only for this resource guide, but personally, so her kindness saved me time in several ways. That's what we women are here to do—love each other. I'd do anything for my friends and vice versa. So don't be afraid to ask. We don't change the world—or find the proper skin care products— alone!

✳ Speaking of women who help other women, Susan Jane Gilman's book *Kiss My Tiara: How to Rule the World as a Smartmouth Goddess* is a Goddess resource, although "Goddess" is simply used in the title as an expression. But this mainstream piece combines self-help and fun, and none does it better.

✳ If you want serious books about Goddess Spirituality and the religion thereof, I'm of course going to recommend mine. *Goddess Initiation: A Practical Celtic Program for Soul-Healing, Self-Fulfillment & Wild Wisdom* is an in-depth program for healing the spirit. I can't ever fully stop being a clown. So the book gets zany occasionally. But readers, including trauma survivors, tell me the humor makes the book non-intimidating. *Be a Goddess! A Guide to Celtic Spells and Wisdom for Self-Healing, Prosperity and Great Sex*, my first book, is also a serious undertaking with bits of silliness. I believe the book provides spiritual answers and tools for change that are practical and relevant.

✳ Back to Jane. I want to give Jane Lind credit for the resources she found. It's so important Goddesses do that for each other instead of being cut-throat competitive. We are crucial resources for each other and must honor others as such. So, Jane also suggests Kama Sutra, sensual products for passion. The line includes luxurious creams, balms, and edible oils. Some of the scents are fabulous. Go to www.shop4love.com.

✳ Most Goddesses feel close to nature and want to take care of Mother Earth. Using organic makeup and skin-care products does this, as well as showing self-respect. A Goddess knows she needn't put nasty chemicals on herself. I asked Jane to find sources and she came up with Cosmetics Without Synthetics at www.allnaturalcosmetics.com and Saffron Rouge, Inc. at http://shop.saffronrouge.com or 866-FACECARE.

✳ Instead of my books which focus on personal application and self-help, you may want to see Carl McColman's *The Complete Idiot's Guide to Paganism,* for an overview of Goddess religion as part of the larger modern pagan scene.

✳ Carl's informative book, *Embracing Jesus and the Goddess,* reveals how Carl reconciled his love for both deities. But he does not ask that practitioners of either religion pursue both paths; the book's main thrust is a thought-provoking challenge that the two communities dialogue. This volume can help non-Goddess worshippers, regardless of their religious choice, better understand the Goddess and those who love her, and help Goddess worshippers come to tolerance and understanding of other religions.

✱ Finally, remember that when looking for additional resources for Goddesses and Goddesses-to-Be, the most important one you can draw on is yourself. Get all the help you need to be you, but do be you. You are absolutely divine. Never forget it.

Your sister Goddess,

Francesca De Grandis

Francesca De Grandis

appendix

the

goddess

pledge

(the "i'm willing

to accept

diamonds as

homage"

manifesto)

I pledge to always know that I'm a Goddess. And if I can't do that, at least to try. And if I can't do that, at least to hope I someday get back to it, and if I can't do that, to make up a good excuse, because that's better than feeling bad about it.

I will honor other women as Goddesses. When I think they couldn't possibly be, I'll hope I'm missing something and find some way, even if it's kind of lame, to acknowledge their divinity. If nothing else, I'll mumble resentfully to myself, "She's a Goddess but, damn, I wish she would get out of my face."

I shall embrace the ruling principle of all Goddesses: love. When I embrace it so loosely that it falls from my grip, I will someday pick it up again, even if for a long time I act like a brat instead.

As a Goddess, it is my duty to love all beings freely. There shall be no strings attached to my love. I shall not demand worship in trade for love, nor dole out love only to those who give me gifts or have the same religion as I. Gifts are nice, however, and if anybody wants to worship me by giving them, I will accept it because it's my duty as a Goddess to accept homage.

I will not use the word love as a disguise for control. If you are my son, daughter, mate, friend, community member, etc., I will not misguidedly believe that love allows me to pressure you into doing what *I* think you should do. If your religion is different from mine, I will not browbeat you with "love" until you worship me.

As for homage, I will accept all gifts, compliments, and offers of help. I will say, "Thank you," instead of refuting kind words said to me.

I will always keep a shrine to Ms. Manners because she is a Goddess: she knows what to do in the most difficult circumstance, realizes that real courtesy is based on kindness instead of on snobbery, and has a really dry sense of humor.

I will love my body in thought and in deed. I will allow no one to disrespect my physical self. When I fail by, for example, thinking someone else is prettier than I am, or succumbing to fashion's absurd standards, or thinking that cellulite actually exists, I will eventually get back to loving my body, accepting that no woman nowadays can ever be completely free of society's unkind messages regarding the female physique.

I will not expect perfection of myself in other areas of my life. I will try to understand that when I think I should, for example, *never* become angry at the stupid things women have to deal with, I'm giving myself a terribly hurtful message: be perfect, and when you're not, beat yourself up for being human.

I will know that when I fail, it is my responsibility to try to change myself. I will also know that when we beat ourselves up for our mistakes, it limits our ability to change.

I will accept others despite their failings. Or at least try not to throw pies at them when they do something wrong. Once again, a Goddess's love is unconditional. And I can throw pies at people if I get a job in a circus or on a TV comedy sitcom. Though not many people throw pies on television anymore, which when I am a more powerful Goddess I will change, because more pie fights will make for a happier world.

I will forgive people their fears, meanness, and other transgressions. If I think forgiveness is wrong, I will discuss this at length with other Goddesses so I'm sure I've made the right decision.

I will listen to my intuition, common sense, and emotions because they will guide me not only in helping myself but in helping others.

I'll respect the little voice in me that tells me when I'm doing something wrong. I'll obey the physical twinge that tells me when my so-called morality or taking the high ground is a disguise for a hurtful act or pettiness.

I will never think there is something I can't achieve. I will never tell anyone else that about themselves.

I will nurture hope in my heart and in the hearts of everyone I meet. Especially the hope that someday there'll be a way not to spend so much time washing dishes.

I will watch out for jealousy in myself and try not to cause it in others. Except by wearing a really stunning outfit, because that's the sort of envy that women just have to cause in each other. And on my wedding day, it's okay if everything about the event causes jealousy.

I will treat the earth as a Mother Goddess who deserves our respect and, now that she is getting older, wants not to be thrown away into the old age home, but tenderly cared for until she can be reborn, as the ever-young Goddess she was meant to be.

I will be honest, and know that if I lie to myself I cannot be truthful with others. Therefore I will never tell myself again that I am dumb or that my breasts are too small, too large, or the wrong shape.

I will understand that women's ways are not always the same as men's and difference is a good thing for everyone involved.

I will tend to those less powerful than I am, whether they are animals, an endangered grove of trees, or people with whom I disagree on the most important of life's issues. Tending people will *not* translate into trying to convert them to my view of life, including, but hardly limited to, my political stance, my religious beliefs, my sexual preference, or my decision that weeding my back yard is their first priority this weekend. A Goddess's care of others is practical: I will help people achieve the human dignity of having basic material needs met.

I will learn to hold a secret when a girlfriend confides in me. If I have to gossip, I will divulge secrets about myself because that's a really fun way to tell tales.

When someone must speak up in the name of those less powerful, I will know that my voice is the voice of a Goddess, and it is my divine duty to say something. But I won't do that thing with the burning bush because that's a Guy-God thing. I don't want my hair to catch on fire.

A Goddess is humble, remembering that all other beings are just as divine. Instead of being creative about finding exceptions to this, I'll persist in learning that every last bit of the Goddess is in every last person, and that she or he is therefore worthy of all the deference and respect that I myself, as a Goddess, merit.

I will attempt to give this deference and respect to everyone, regardless of how they might differ from me in lifestyle, hairstyle, or opinion on revivals. (I mean, bell bottoms, modesty, The Monkees, and morality have all been revived at least once. So, let's not make an issue out of any of them.)

I will not make *deference and respect* mean saying or doing something really yucky to someone so that I can feel morally superior while actually being mean.

I will laugh a lot and never chide another for expressing joy. I respect the pleasure of this material plane and honor everyone's right to it.

I will not be so greedy that there is not enough abundance left over for others to have their fair share of the pleasure.

I will learn that serving others and sharing my goods with them, with no agenda for personal gain or religious conversion, is necessary for my happiness, although it makes no logical sense. When I am trying to heal myself of fear, anger, self-defeating beliefs, anxiety, depression, and other inner problems, and nothing else has worked, I will do something for someone else, because that might be the final healing step that's needed. Even if it makes no logical sense.

I will tell myself often, "I am a Goddess, I am a Goddess, I am a Goddess."

I will always believe in the future, knowing that someday, when all Goddesses have taken this pledge and found their full power, we shall be able to convene, and, sharing our divine wisdom, find a substitute for the underwire bra.

So be it.

Acknowledgments:

I especially want to thank Iyanla Vanzant and her staff for helping me create the "What Goddess Are You?" show on which I appeared. It was one of the inspirations for this book.

Huge chocolate thanks to the following people:

My agents—Elizabeth Pomada and Michael Larsen—as well as my Sourcebooks editor, Deborah Werksman, who believed in this insane project as *viable* lunacy, then did the innumerable things needed to make it so. Ditto Sourcebooks's Susie Benton, Jill Amack, Michelle Schoob, and Megan Dempster. Copy editor Heidi Bell could not have done a better job. Todd Barrett typed the proposal. Sara Shopkow edited it. Janaya did a quick 'n' dirty edit of the revised proposal. Bob W. contributed typing, related activities, and promises of sexual favors. Danyea S., typing sprite, worked at assorted clerical duties. My test-readers, Jane Lind, Candace Finn, and Laurey Shumaker, told me when the manuscript lacked fun, effectiveness, and other necessities. Kush and Phoebe kept me writing. The Pink Bunny Tribe, aka the friends who saw me through my recent illness, kept me healthy enough in body and spirit *to* write. I'm blessed that there are too many tribe members to name, because without such quantity of care-taking I might not have survived the illness, but there are some people who gave so crucially that I must mention them: my doctor, Larry Becker, and his wife, Ginger Ashworth, as well as Thom Fowler, Janaya, Mark Alexander, Brian Peterson, Ken Vinson, Angela Kitchens, Denise Ray, Shirley K., Annie Sprinkle, Adrienne Admundsen, Catherine Kubu, Stephanie Fay, Lynn Stewart, Todd Barrett, Vanna Z. Red, Kathleen Marshall, Dawnwalker, Carl McColman, Russell Williams, Kush, Z. Budapest, Laura Gail Grohe, Kae Kohl, Elizabeth Pomada, Mike Larsen, and last alphabetically but deep in my heart, Phoebe Wray, who understands the fine art of friendship, with all its discipline, effort, joy, revelry, and compassion. Moving on: My incredibly supportive students and readers make all my work possible and worth it—especially Dawn Walker, Kathi Somers, Ken Vinson, Angela Kitchens, Geoff Cohen, Morgaina, Kae Kohl, and Scott Schulz. Deborah Stafford is my irreplaceable and invaluable "alter ego, dark twin, and dragon at the gate." "The fellowship" has given me my life, sanity, and joy. And my Divine Mother and Father give me *all* things I have.

the modern goddess' guide to life

About the Author

Francesca De Grandis is an interfaith pastoral counselor and traditional spiritual healer, focusing her classes and counseling on helping others find prosperity, create their own destiny, and make a difference in the world. She lives in San Francisco, where she teaches Goddess Spirituality and interfaith spirituality locally as well as through international tele-seminars (classes by telephone). She provides spiritual counseling (psychic readings) by telephone for people all over the world. *The Wiccan & Faerie Grimoire of Francesca De Grandis*, at www.well.com/user/zthirdrd/WiccanMiscellany.html, is an award-winning resource. She is the author of *Goddess Initiation: A Practical Celtic Program for Soul Healing, Self-Fulfillment & Wild Wisdom* (HarperSanFrancisco) and *Be A Goddess! A Guide to Celtic Spells and Wisdom for Self-Healing, Prosperity and Great Sex* (HarperSanFrancisco). In her free time—what free time?—Francesca edits and teaches writing and publishing classes.

Ms. De Grandis can be reached via her website or at 415-750-1205; P.O. Box 210307, San Francisco, California 94121.

Brian Peterson

the modern goddess' guide to life